# PICTURES AND PREMIERES

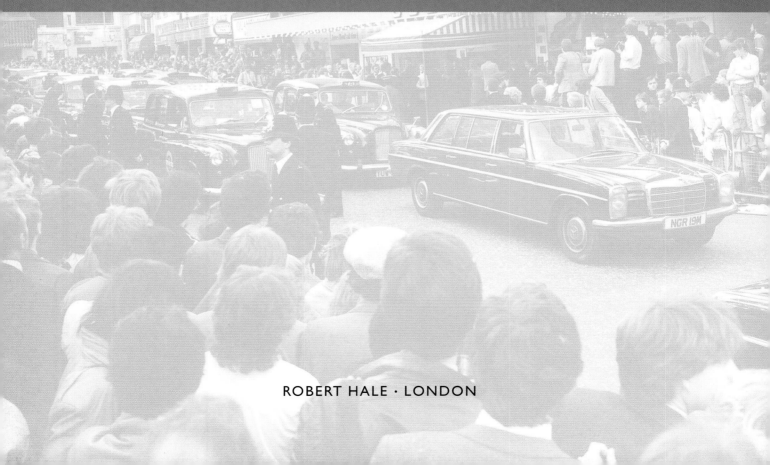

# PICTURES
## AND
# PREMIERES

### HARRY MYERS, JOHN WILLIS & GARETH OWEN

Foreword by Sir ROGER MOORE KBE

**ROBERT HALE · LONDON**

© Harry Myers, John Willis & Gareth Owen 2007
First published in Great Britain 2007

ISBN 978 0 7090 8329 0

Robert Hale Limited
Clerkenwell House
Clerkenwell Green
London EC1R 0HT

The right of Harry Myers, John Willis and Gareth Owen to be identified
as authors of this work has been asserted by them in accordance with the
Copyright, Designs and Patents Act 1988

A catalogue record for this book is available from the British Library

2 4 6 8 10 9 7 5 3 1

Design and typesetting by Paul Saunders

Colour Separation by Tenon & Polert Colour Scanning Ltd

Printed through New Era Printing Company Limited, China

# CONTENTS

# ACKNOWLEDGEMENTS

There are so many people to thank, not only for helping in this book, but in my career. Top of the list is my wife Anne, followed by my children Scott and Ashley. Their support and love continues to drive me.

Scott and I are deeply indebted to Rex Features who now own the copyright in the vast majority of the images in this book, which were taken during a period of over sixty years. This leading agency's unstinted assistance and supply of many prints has proved invaluable and we would in particular like to thank Frank, Elizabeth, John, Mike and Sue Selby who run the business of Rex Features. The publication of our book is accordingly in no small way attributable to the Selby family.

My grateful thanks are also extended to Barry Cerasoli at Rex who helped so efficiently with pulling copies of photos from the archive, and for being a great friend.

Without John Willis and Gareth Owen I would still be staring at boxes and cupboards full of photographs at home, not quite knowing what to do with them. They, above any others, have made this book possible and I remain indebted to them for their belief, patience and for making sense of my ramblings.

My sincere thanks also goes to Sir Roger Moore for writing such a gracious foreword and for help in identifying some of the people featured in the book where my memory failed; to my dear, and sadly departed, secretary Marjory Stephenson who was, for so many years, my right hand and caption writer; to Lynne Willis, ever supportive wife of John; to Chris Hilton and all at the Odeon Leicester Square; to Lesley Pollinger and all at Pollinger Ltd; to the staff at the CTBF in London; and everyone at Robert Hale Ltd.

Finally to the TRH the Royal Family and the multitudes of film stars who have graced the red carpet in front of my, and my son's, camera … I thank you so sincerely for allowing me to carry out a job I loved.

HARRY MYERS

# FOREWORD

I must have attended scores of premieres over the years – something of an occupational hazard, you might say. The buzz of excitement is fantastic. The crowds gather early in Leicester Square, the red carpet is rolled out … ah, the magic of movies!

If I'm honest, I much prefer attending other people's premieres. I don't feel nearly so nervous, nor do I need to worry that, if the audience don't like the film, I'll never work again.

One familiar face at many, if not most, of the premieres I attended in London was Harry Myers. His friendly smile stood out in an ocean of flash bulbs and lenses. He was never intrusive or pushy. Always immaculately dressed in black tie and tuxedo, he was highly regarded and respected by everyone. How times have changed.

I am delighted that Harry has finally put together around 300 of his and Scott's terrific photographs in this book, along with many of his anecdotes. He's even been kind enough to feature me in a few.

See you at the next premiere!

*Roger Moore*

Sir Roger Moore KBE

Sir Roger and Lady Moore attend the 59th Royal Film Performance, *The Chronicles of Narnia: The Lion, the Witch and the Wardrobe* in November 2005 at the Royal Albert Hall

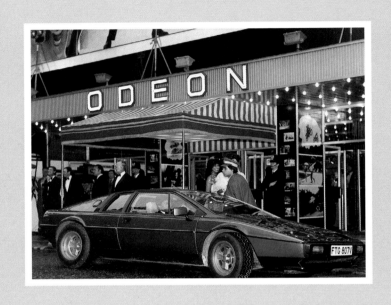

# INTRODUCTION

'I've got through an awful lot of dinner suits over the years!' exclaims Harry Myers.

For over five decades no major London premiere was complete without Harry's camera. The popular cockney, born in the Clerkenwell Road, has photographed virtually every major film star and movie mogul to have set foot in the capital. He captured perfectly the ballyhoo and razzamatazz surrounding their films. From Fred Astaire to Hollywood pioneer Adolph Zukor, from the Beatles to John Wayne, if they were in London, Harry was on hand to ensure that their photographs graced the breakfast table of every newspaper reader around the world.

A flick through some of the thousands upon thousands of photographs Harry has taken over the decades illustrates the esteem in which British audiences were held by the major motion picture studios. To their delight, stars lionized in Hollywood were prepared for long sea voyages to visit England and shake hands with HM the Queen and other members of the royal family.

Since covering his first, and *the* first, Royal Film Performance in 1946 – *A Matter of Life and Death* – when he was just an 18-year-old fledging photographer, Harry, along with his son Scott in more recent years, has covered every single RFP and countless other royal charity events. They have brought him into contact with, and won the respect of, the Queen, the Queen Mother, the Duke of Edinburgh, Prince Charles and the late Diana, Princess of Wales, and Princess Margaret and her former husband Lord Snowdon. Ever present, though seemingly never in the way, Harry undertook his job with professionalism, pride and relish.

After leaving school, aged 13, Harry went straight into his first job. 'I decided I did not want to be evacuated from London so I asked my head teacher if there was any point in my staying on in school since I would be 14 the following February and legally allowed to leave. The job was glazing prints for newspapers at the London News Agency, which in 1904 was the first photographic agency to be established in Fleet Street.

'My job entailed placing wet prints on a hot revolving drum which then came off dry and glossy. At the time I didn't have any interest in photography, but the job did encourage me to look at pictures and I developed an appreciation for what was good and what was bad. I didn't realize it, but I was actually getting a terrific grounding in what was to become my future career. One day when I was 17 my boss came in and said there was a rush job in Lower Regent Street. I got on the bus with this heavy plate camera and huge flash apparatus and went to photograph the chairman of the gas council, visiting a showroom.'

One of Harry's earliest memories is of running across London during the Blitz with prints sent in from the war zones to be censored by the Ministry of Information. These included ninety photographs depicting the horrors of Belsen concentration camp in Germany. Only two were passed for publication.

Having, by this time, taken up photography himself, Harry vividly remembers walking around the capital on the night World War II ended, taking photographs of well-known buildings such as Tower Bridge and Big Ben lit up again after six years of blackout. He sold them to his agency, and they quickly recognized his talent as a photographer. Harry meanwhile quickly recognized this could be a way to make a decent pound or two! Harry became the agency's society photographer. Any occasion from weddings, balls, christenings and so forth, Harry would be there. It was no surprise that 'society events' would one day combine with Harry's other great interest in life – movies.

'Thus I found myself back in 1946 feeling a little lost among 40,000 people in Leicester Square waiting for the King and Queen to arrive for the first Royal Command Film Performance of *A Matter of Life and Death*. I remember I was told to capture far more than just the royals. We were looking to get the producers and stars to show a real sense of a historic occasion.' Harry, resplendent in his dinner suit did later admit to having been so nervous after covering his first royal premiere that 'you could squeeze the perspiration out of it'.

'Those were the days when we were covering premieres with 5x4 Speed Graphic cameras,' he says. 'I used to have about fifty double dark slides which I carried with me over my shoulder. I had to work by television lights, no flash, which presented quite a problem.'

After eighteen years Harry Myers left the London News Agency to form his own company, PIC Photos Ltd, and strengthen a long relationship with Wardour Street, then the centre of the film distribution business. As glamorous as premieres can be, it was often a pressurized race against time for the keen photographer, building his fledgling photographic agency. 'Columbia Pictures would, for example, want seven prints of 100 exposures of a film premiere to promote the film to cinema owners, in order for them to book it. And they wanted them ASAP. We'd be printing and captioning throughout the night,' Harry reflects. Sometimes he wouldn't arrive home until five or six in the morning. He'd take a shower, have a cup of tea, take the children to school and settle down to read the newspapers over breakfast, many of which featured his photographs. 'We had a free hand with the images so I would run up and down Fleet Street selling to the national newspapers the latest pictures of Judy Garland, John Wayne, James Stewart and so on.'

Capturing not only the mood and atmosphere of the time, Harry was, inadvertently, cataloguing the fashion and changing face of the decades he worked through. 'In the early days of the Royal Film Performances, the women would wear diamonds and furs, while the men wore white tie and tails, often with medals,' laments Harry. 'Old school glamour was very much the order of the day. After the mid-1960s all that changed. Things became less formal and much more casual. Dinner suits and tiaras were out. In fact I did later often wonder if some people had brushed their hair, let alone thought about what they were wearing. The world was changing and the face of premieres – certainly aided by The Beatles – changed too.'

But one thing never changed through the decades. 'At each and every premiere,' says Harry, 'I noticed just how much in awe of the Royal patron the stars were, in particular the Queen. No matter how famous they were, they held her in total reverence. Maybe it's because they knew that no matter how great was *their* fame, they could never touch that of our Queen.' Harry captured that reverence on a great many occasions, and often found the stars would request copies of his photographs featuring them meeting royalty. 'I have lost count of the number of times when I've been watching a television interview with a star in their home, and in the background on a piano or a table caught sight of one of my photographs. I'm actually enormously proud'.

In the late 1990s, after five happy decades behind the lens, Harry decided to retire from the business and sell his library to the respected Fleet Street Agency,

Rex Features, leaving his son Scott to occupy his spot on the red carpet at premieres.

The idea of compiling a book of some of his favourite photographs was something that had cropped up occasionally over the years. It was always quickly dismissed for reasons of time. However, now enjoying his retirement, and after constant badgering from friends and colleagues, Harry succumbed. Just skimming the surface of his archives has thrown up a remarkable pictorial record of a former age of protocol and elegance and reveals a fascinating glimpse of a royal family ageing graciously over the decades. Short-listing 300 of Harry and his son Scott's favourite photographs for this book was an unenviable task. It was not a case of 'what should go in' but rather a case of 'what can't we squeeze in'.

JOHN WILLIS & GARETH OWEN

# ONE

# THE NAME'S BOND, JAMES BOND

Everyone knows the name. Everyone knows the number.

With twenty-one entries to date, the James Bond series of films made by Eon Productions is the most successful in the world. The latest, *Casino Royale* (2006) took over 400 million dollars in its first month on release, making it the highest grossing and most financially successful film in the franchise's history. It also became the first 007 adventure to have a premiere in China.

It all began in 1953 when, on the eve of his marriage, Ian Fleming penned what he termed the 'spy novel to end all spy novels', the aforementioned *Casino Royale*. It became a bestseller and ensured thirteen further adventure volumes, up until his death in 1964. After selling the rights to his first book in 1954, a forgettable live TV production followed with Climax Theatre casting American Barry Nelson as 'Jimmy Bond' against Peter Lorre's LeChiffre. The rights, incidentally, eventually ended up with former agent and then a producer Charles K. Feldman who, at the height of Bondmania in the mid 1960s, produced a spoof version of the book starring Peter Sellers, David Niven and Orson Welles.

Fleming courted several producers in the 1950s and into the early 1960s, in the hope of establishing a film series of his books, to no avail. At one point The Rank Organisation optioned *Moonraker* though never exercised it.

Then an enterprising young Irish producer named Kevin McClory became involved and collaborated on a few film treatments with Fleming. Ultimately nothing came of them, although Fleming used one of the treatments as the basis for his novel *Thunderball*. A lengthy court case ensued with McClory being awarded a share of royalties and the film rights.

In 1961, a Canadian producer named Harry Saltzman, who had enjoyed considerable success with movies in the UK such as *Saturday Night and Sunday Morning* and *The Entertainer*, did a deal with Fleming and bought an option on the books. Unable to raise any finance Saltzman's option was about to expire when he was introduced to American producer Albert 'Cubby' Broccoli. Like Harry Saltzman, Broccoli had enjoyed some success with producing movies in Britain – *Cockleshell Heroes*, *The Black Knight*, and *The Trials of Oscar Wilde* – and had expressed an interest in the Bond novels, but did not pursue them when he was informed the rights were not available.

Saltzman had the rights. Broccoli had access to money. They formed a partnership, and founded Eon Productions to make a series of Bond films. Broccoli hurriedly set up a meeting with United Artists and clinched a multi-picture deal. The first was to be *Thunderball*, but with legal wranglings ongoing between Fleming and McClory, focus was shifted into turning Fleming's novel *Dr No* into the first James Bond film adventure. With a budget of $1 million, and a relatively unknown named Sean Connery in the lead, the film opened in the UK on 5 October 1962. It went on to gross $59.5 million worldwide. A success by anyone's measure.

A sequel was planned, and when President Kennedy named *From Russia with Love* among his ten favourite books of all time, producers Broccoli and Saltzman found it timely to choose this as the follow-up to the cinematic debut of 007. Greater success followed with *Goldfinger* and *Thunderball* – the latter still being, in real terms, the most financially successfully entry in the series. Bondmania was at its height by the mid 1960s. The films' formula was simple: great escapism, wonderful locations, gadgets and, of course, beautiful girls. The likes of which had never been experienced before.

'I never made up my mind who Bond is,' said Cubby Broccoli once. 'Sometimes I think it's very dramatic but mostly it's comedy. One thing I know for certain – it's entertainment.'

From being relatively unknown, Sean Connery was launched to superstardom and was able to accept a number of acting assignments between Bond films, making him one of the busiest actors in the business. However, by the time of his fifth Bond, *You Only Live Twice* in 1967, Connery was tiring of the role and, in particular, the media frenzy that surrounded him wherever he went. It reached boiling point when, on location, photographers followed Connery into the lavatory when he was on location in Japan. He announced that he would be leaving the role after his fifth outing.

After a much-hyped search, the new 007 was confirmed as former model and chocolate commercial actor George Lazenby. After receiving bad advice, Lazenby refused to commit to more than one film, feeling he would make his name and move on from what he thought of as 'Connery's gig'. He now admits it was the worst decision of his life. However, it did lead to Sean Connery returning to the role of 007 for *Diamonds Are Forever*, before he said 'never again'. In 1973 he handed the famous Walther PPK over to Roger Moore, who had achieved considerable international fame as The Saint. Moore made seven highly successful Bond adventures before retiring from the role in 1986.

Timothy Dalton took over for two outings in 1987 and 1989 before, in 1995, and following a lengthy legal case between the producers and MGM, Pierce Brosnan signed up for four films. He rejuvenated the franchise and each of his films out grossed the previous with his last, *Die Another Day* (2002) holding the box-office record … that is, until Bond mark 6, Daniel Craig, debuted in *Casino Royale*!

Bond is back, and very much here to stay!

## THE JAMES BOND FILMS

| | |
|---|---|
| *Dr. No* (1962) | *For Your Eyes Only* (1981) |
| *From Russia with Love* (1963) | *Octopussy* (1983) |
| *Goldfinger* (1964) | *A View to a Kill* (1985) |
| *Thunderball* (1965) | *The Living Daylights* (1987) |
| *You Only Live Twice* (1967) | *Licence to Kill* (1989) |
| *On Her Majesty's Secret Service* (1969) | *Goldeneye* (1995) |
| *Diamonds Are Forever* (1971) | *Tomorrow Never Dies* (1997) |
| *Live and Let Die* (1973) | *The World Is Not Enough* (1999) |
| *The Man with the Golden Gun* (1974) | *Die Another Day* (2002) |
| *The Spy who Loved Me* (1977) | *Casino Royale* (2006) |
| *Moonraker* (1979) | |

© REX FEATURES

© REX FEATURES

I had quite a lot to do with Sean Connery when he was first signed as James Bond. I lived in a flat in Regent's Park and Sean lived just behind. Perhaps it was because of our close proximity that Roy McGregor, Eon Productions publicity director, asked me in to photograph Sean. As he was a relative unknown, Eon was very keen to generate as much publicity for him as possible. I was wondering what we might do for a theme. I asked Sean what car he had. He said, proudly, 'a Porsche'. Aha, I thought, that will make an interesting set-up – James Bond in his high-powered car. I asked him to drive it around the area and I'd take some shots of him with it. Well, it was a rather old model and had quite a lot of dents in to say the least! Not quite what I'd imagined, but they still proved very popular all the same.

I then went with Sean to London's famous Savile Row, to photograph him being fitted for his new suits. The photos appeared in a lot of the national newspapers. It was after that when Roy McGregor asked if I would like to be unit photographer on the first 007 film, *Dr No*, starting with six weeks in Jamaica. Unfortunately, I couldn't accept because I was booked to go to Moscow as official photographer to the British Trade Fair.

Ian Fleming, creator of James Bond, in a rare candid shot. This was one of only two occasions I met the great writer; it was at the post-screening party of *Dr No*. Believe it or not, there wasn't an actual premiere, rather just a gala opening screening

However, I did photograph Sean boarding his flight to Jamaica for the first day of shooting of *Dr No*. His reading material, in hand, was Tennessee Williams' *Three Players of a Summer Game*

Anita Ekberg, Sean Connery and his *Dr No* co-star, Zena Marshall at the film's post-screening party in Audley Square. Zena Marshall told me that Sean had asked her to accompany him as he and his then wife, Diane Cilento, had just had a big argument and she refused to attend!

The second James Bond film, *From Russia with Love*, didn't receive a premiere either, just a gala screening. Here I captured the crowds outside the Odeon Leicester Square queuing for tickets. Those were the days when cars could drive around the square

My second encounter with Ian Fleming. Here he is flanked by Harry Saltzman (*left*) and Cubby Broccoli, the Bond producers. This shot was taken on 10 October 1963 at the Odeon Leicester Square – the opening night of *From Russia with Love*

This time Sean Connery's wife did accompany him! Here the Bond producers pose with Sean and Diane Cilento in the lounge at the Odeon Leicester Square, again on the opening night of the second Bond film. Sean's parents were there too, they'd travelled all the way from Edinburgh to share in their son's success. A lovely couple

By the time the third Bond film came around, *Goldfinger*, the hype and excitement was huge. A proper premiere was called for! One of the first couples to arrive at the Odeon Leicester Square was German actor Gert Frobe and his wife Beate Bach. He, of course, played the titular villain and far from being cold-hearted and humourless like his character, in real life he was a wonderfully jovial man

Shirley Eaton played the ill-fated Jill Masterson in *Goldfinger* and will be forever remembered for being painted gold. What an iconic image that was. Pity I never photographed it. I knew Shirley quite well, as her husband Colin Rowe was a great friend of mine

As more stars arrived for the premiere, things outside were getting rather hairy and with the crowds bursting through, extra police were summoned with some urgency. Bondmania was here!

As the movie was quite possibly the most anticipated of the year, the producers were very keen that no one should see it before the premiere. They therefore arranged for the film prints to be delivered via armoured truck on the evening of the premiere, and once the strong box had been taken inside the foyer of the theatre, four rather beautiful ladies unpacked the gold cans and carried them through. The ruse was later copied by the BBC when the famous episode of *Dallas* was screened, with JR's killer identified

© REX FEATURES

*Goldfinger* was big, but the next 007 adventure, *Thunderball*, was even bigger. It marked the very peak of Bondmania. There was more action, more exotic locations, and more beautiful ladies. Here are the four leading actresses: Mollie Peters, Claudine Auger, Martine Beswicke and Luciana Paluzzi, toasting success to the movie at the Odeon Leicester Square

*Thunderball's* producer Kevin McClory is pictured here with heiress Bobo Segrist, whom he later married, and Luciana Paluzzi

© REX FEATURES

Villain of the piece, and the peace, Adolfo Celi pictured with Mrs Charles Berman (her husband was director of publicity for United Artists, the film's distributor)

Sean Connery and Diane Cilento dance the night away at the *Thunderball* post-premiere party, which was held at Claridges. Note Sean has ditched his collar and tie at this stage

© REX FEATURES

After Sean Connery quit, the search was on for a replacement 007. Months of press speculation culminated in George Lazenby being unveiled to the press on Monday 7 October 1968 at the Dorchester Hotel, where I snapped this photo of Lazenby enjoying a cigarette. There was a genuine air of surprise at the choice of an unknown actor to replace Connery. Despite him being a model and actor in a popular series of chocolate commercials, no one really knew who he was but everyone was really intrigued as to how he planned to take over from Connery

© REX FEATURES

Roll on a year, and George Lazenby's first – and some say the best – Bond film, *On Her Majesty's Secret Service* was complete and premiered in London on 18 December 1969. It was the first and only time Lazenby met his public, arriving here with his co-star Diana Rigg. Lazenby turned up with decidedly un-Bond like shoulder length hair and a thick beard. There had been many stories of the star disagreeing with the producers and director throughout the shoot, and of him saying he was not going to make a second film. The producers were keen to quash all of those stories this night; but in his arrogant style, Lazenby decided he would do things on his terms. It was clear they were parting company

Director Peter Hunt, who had served as editor on the preceding Bond films, made his debut with *On Her Majesty's Secret Service*. He is pictured here with Marjory Cornelius, his great friend and costume designer on the film

© REX FEATURES

Following Lazenby's departure, the producers were desperately keen to persuade Sean Connery to return. Making him an offer he couldn't refuse, Eon and their backers United Artists, secured him to star in *Diamonds Are Forever*. However, he then said 'never again' and moved on from Bond. The hunt was on, yet again, for a new 007. In 1972 it was announced that former Saint and Persuader, Roger Moore had been contracted. His first film was *Live and Let Die*. There was huge anticipation and excitement, particularly on premiere day as the gathered crowds indicate that afternoon

The great John Barry with his companion for the evening premiere of Roger Moore's second Bond film, *The Man with the Golden Gun*, on 19 December 1974. John composed the majority of the Bond scores, and my links with him actually go back to his father, Jack Prendergast, who owned and ran cinemas up in Yorkshire. Every year they would attend the Cinema Exhibitors' Association convention

© REX FEATURES

© REX FEATURES

The delightful Lulu, who sung the title theme for *The Man with the Golden Gun*

It's interesting to note that there were five performances per day, to meet demand, with a late show at weekends

The Odeon foyer, and Prince Phillip meets Kerima, wife of director Guy Hamilton, who is standing to her left. I first met Kerima when she starred in Carol Reed's film *Outcast of the Islands* in 1952. I was asked to take some photographs for the production company, British Lion. Guy Hamilton was assistant director on that film, and that's where he first met Kerima. They married soon afterwards and have been together ever since. Just next to Guy is Jacqueline Saltzman, Harry's wife, and looking over her shoulder is her son Steven

© REX FEATURES

◀ **OPPOSITE**

Here he is at last! Roger Moore, the third actor to portray 007 on the big screen. This sweltering hot evening on 7 July 1977 marked the premiere of *The Spy Who Loved Me*, arguably Roger's best Bond adventure. He is pictured with his leading lady Barbara Bach, and the film's director, Lewis Gilbert, who is one of the most genial and lovely film directors in the business. He always seemed genuinely surprised whenever anyone asked to take his photograph

**ABOVE**

The distinguished German actor Curt Jurgens, who played the villain Stromberg, arrives at the Odeon with his soon-to-be-wife, Margie Schmitz. At this time, Jurgens lived in Gstaad, Switzerland. He invited Roger Moore out to stay after filming, and as Roger was contemplating having to go tax-exile around then due to the prohibitive rate of income tax, he fell in love with and duly moved to Gstaad. Jurgens also kept a villa in the south of France and was famed for throwing a huge party at every Cannes Film Festival for the German press in attendance. Needless to say, he always received favourable press in his home country

An interesting moment with Barbara Bach and Roger Moore. I'm not quite sure what they were discussing. Answers on a postcard!

Arriving at *The Spy who Loved Me* premiere is producer Cubby Broccoli, making his first solo Bond film after splitting from Harry Saltzman in 1975, with his wife Dana. Their daughter Barbara was accompanied by family friend Dodi Fayed, who was then making a name for himself as a film producer

© REX FEATURES

When I first met Richard Kiel, I was a little taken aback. At 7ft 2in, he's quite a size. However, he is one of the gentlest, kindest, most intelligent and good-humoured actors I've ever met. Here he is being presented to Princess Anne. To his left is Oscar winning production designer Ken Adam, a regular Bond contributor, and Michael G. Wilson who was credited as special assistant to Cubby Broccoli. Michael subsequently became executive producer, followed by co-producer and writer on Roger's later and Timothy Dalton's films. He subsequently, with his step-sister Barbara Broccoli, went on to produce Pierce Brosnan's and Daniel Craig's Bond films. Just behind Princess Anne's head you can see John Glen. John was second unit director and editor, and such was the success of the ski-jump that he directed in the pre-titles sequence that he was brought back for *Moonraker* in the same capacity, and then hired to direct five 007 films in the 1980s

As the next film was called *Moonraker*, it seemed only fitting to have one of the model shuttles attend the opening. Here onlookers crowd Leicester Square to catch a glimpse

Roger Moore is sporting a beard for his next film, *North Sea Hijack*, which he had just started filming. Here, meeting Prince Philip, is his former wife Luisa, producer Cubby Broccoli and his wife Dana.

On 24 June 1981, *For Your Eyes Only* premiered. One of the supporting actresses was a fantastically beautiful lady named Cassandra Harris. She was accompanied by her husband, a struggling young actor named Pierce Brosnan. No one seemed interested in the couple, and I was the only photographer to take a picture. Funny how things turn out, isn't it?

© REX FEATURES

Along with the beautiful girls, Bond films are also renowned for terrific gadgets. In *For Your Eyes Only* most of his gadgetry was housed in a Lotus Esprit. One of the cars used in the film was driven in to Leicester Square on the rather drizzly June evening, to greet the crowds

After splitting from Cubby Broccoli in the mid 1970s, Harry Saltzman's career never really recovered. His wife Jacqueline also became ill and succumbed to cancer soon afterwards. It was a very dark time for him. However, at Topol's bidding, Cubby Broccoli invited his former partner to the premiere of *For Your Eyes Only*, and Harry attended with his daughter Hilary and son Christopher. It was a very emotional reunion for the two producers, and Saltzman admitted to being extremely proud and happy to be in attendance

© REX FEATURES

Pictured arriving at the premiere of *For Your Eyes Only*, just about a month before they married, Prince Charles and Lady Diana Spencer were the most talked about couple in the media. They arrived with Princess Margaret and together certainly upstaged the stars of the film

Roger Moore's sixth outing as James Bond was in *Octopussy*.
As the slogans declared, it was James Bond's all time high

Stalwarts of the series, Lois Maxwell and Desmond Llewelyn, better known as Miss Moneypenny and gadget master Q were the films' longest serving cast members

Mr and Mrs Roger Moore chat with Prince Charles. Their daughter, Deborah, who herself went on to appear in a future Bond film *Die Another Day*, is standing just over her father's right shoulder

BELOW
The film's leading lady, Maud Adams, standing to the left of director John Glen, talks enthusiastically with Prince Charles, as Princess Diana greets others in the line-up

Mr and Mrs Roger Moore
share a moment with
Princess Diana

© REX FEATURES

© REX FEATURES

**LEFT**
In 1983 Sean Connery was
persuaded to return to the
role of James Bond by
producer Kevin McClory in a
loose remake of *Thunderball*.
With him having previously
declared 'never again' to play
Bond, Micheline Connery,
pictured here with her
husband, and Ringo Starr and
Barbara Bach, told Sean to
'never say never again'. And so
the movie was titled *Never Say
Never Again*. The film premiered
at the Warner cinema in
Leicester Square

In 1985 Roger Moore made his last film as 007, *A View to a Kill*. Here Prince Charles chats with the members of Duran Duran, who performed the film's title song

© REX FEATURES

© REX FEATURES

**LEFT**
A rare reunion. Three former James Bonds together in 2002: Roger Moore, George Lazenby and Timothy Dalton. Dalton only made two outings as 007, as his third was cancelled when the producers entered in to a lengthy legal case with MGM, their backers. He remains hugely popular

© REX FEATURES

Director of *Die Another Day*, Lee Tamahori is pictured here by my son Scott, with Halle Berry (who played Jinx in the movie) on his left, and Rachel Grant (who played Peaceful Fountains of Desire)

◄ OPPOSITE

In 1995, the fifth actor to play 007 was unveiled to the world. He was Pierce Brosnan who, some fourteen years earlier, I photographed arriving at the premiere of *For Your Eyes Only* as an unknown actor. Now my son Scott was photographing him as James Bond, alongside his co-star Halle Berry in *Die Another Day* – Brosnan's fourth film in the role, and most financially successful. As the Odeon Leicester Square was booked solid, the producers decided to stage the biggest film premiere London had ever seen by

transforming the Royal Albert Hall into a cinema for the night. The exterior was decorated to resemble the ice palace featured in the film, and a huge after-show party was held across in Hyde Park. The film marked the fortieth anniversary of the series, and former Bonds George Lazenby, Roger Moore and Timothy Dalton also attended. Her Majesty the Queen and HRH Prince Philip attended, and were delighted to learn that the premiere raised over £500,000 for the Cinema and Television Benevolent Fund (CTBF)

© REX FEATURES

After securing the rights to Ian Fleming's first book, *Casino Royale*, the producers decided it was time to take Bond back to basics. As such, a new, younger actor was needed. After many months of rumour and speculation, Daniel Craig was announced on October 14th 2005 as the sixth actor to take over the famed licence to kill. He was given a very rough ride by the press and fans, and criticized before he even started filming. Just over a year later, he silenced all of his doubters when his debut 007 film premiered. It was the chosen film for the sixtieth Royal Film Performance, and was attended by the Queen and Prince Philip. To accommodate the demand the whole of Leicester Square was taken over, and three cinemas: the Odeon, Odeon West End and Empire held simultaneous screenings. It was the biggest premiere ever staged in London accommodating 4,200 cinemagoers. It raised over £300,000 for the CTBF. Daniel Craig attended with his girlfriend Satsuki Mitchell, whilst leading lady Eva Green adopted a rather gothic-looking dress for the evening

© REX FEATURES

ABOVE

That's me, Harry Myers, attending my sixtieth Royal Film performance with *Casino Royale*. I was, however, off duty that night, leaving my son Scott to handle the picture taking. This photo of me in Leicester Square was taken by my friend Marilyn Dennis, Chairwoman of the Field End Photographic Society

An interesting shot by my son Scott. Here is Sean Connery with his brother Neil, a sometime actor, who always likes to introduce himself as 'Sean Connery's brother'

**ABOVE LEFT**
Remember the golden girl,
Shirley Eaton? Well, here she
is again, looking as beautiful
as ever, and pictured with
Barbara Broccoli

**ABOVE RIGHT**
My son Scott captured this
fun shot of Barbara Broccoli
with Timothy Dalton at a
Leicester Square screening

Can it be the same young
girl? Barbara Broccoli,
pictured here by me on her
seventh birthday

The Broccoli clan at Barbara's third birthday party. *Left to Right:* Cubby, Michael, Dana and Tina, Barbara and Tony. Prior to his great James Bond success, I met film producer Albert 'Cubby' Broccoli in London during the 1950s when he and his then producing partner Irving Allen had a company called Warwick Films. They most famously produced a number of pictures with Alan Ladd such as *Red Beret*, *The Black Knight* and *Cockleshell Heroes*. It was around *Cockleshell Heroes* time that Cubby, through his publicity manager Euan Lloyd, asked me to go to his house to photograph him and his wife – his second wife Nedra, who sadly died of cancer soon afterwards. That was really the beginning of our long relationship. Whenever there was a party at the house, Cubby asked me to go and photograph it and years later when he was making the Bond films, and married to Dana, he asked me to photograph their young daughter Barbara's birthday party. Now Barbara produces the Bond films, and remains as sweet and charming as when I first met her as a child

© REX FEATURES

© REX FEATURES

The only other film which Cubby Broccoli made during the Bond years was a children's film, an adaptation of Ian Fleming's *Chitty Chitty Bang Bang*. Here Cubby and Dana are presented to the Queen on 16 December 1968 at the Odeon Leicester Square. Note the TV camera. My old pal Steve Minchin who directed the televising of the premieres could always be heard to shout, 'Harry will you get that white-haired head of yours out of my bloody camera shot'

# TWO

✦

# THE BEATLES

Beatlemania entered the English language on 2 November, 1963.

It was a term coined by the London *Daily Mirror* when they reviewed one of the Fab Four's early concerts in Cheltenham. Beatlemania was also the working title of the first Beatles film but it was later changed to *Hard Day's Night*.

'My old friend Michael Winner told me he had tried to get a film together with Paul, George, John and Ringo,' says Harry Myers. 'He offered £40,000 to secure a deal with their manager Brian Epstein. It was rejected in favour of one with United Artists that was actually a three-picture deal, paying, I believe, £5,000 for the first film, £10,000 and £15,000 for the third. This was nowhere near Winner's original bid for just one film and so Winner contacted the American-based company's UK production executive, Bud Ornstein, and asked if he could direct it, only to be told that Richard Lester had been signed.' Perceiving the film to be a low-budget 'quickie', Ornstein appointed ex-publicity chief, Walter Shenson as the producer, receiving 50 per cent of the film's net profits.

'Following the success of *Hard Day's Night*,' adds Harry, 'Shenson wanted his friend Ornstein to share in the profits for setting up the deal but United Artist's executive Arthur Krim rejected the deal, saying that as an executive of UA Ornstein could not expect a producer's royalty. That film – together with others featuring the Beatles: *Help!*, *Let It Be* and *Yellow Submarine*, plus *The*

*Magical Mystery Tour* – went on to make world-wide fortunes, as did Walter Shenson, who became a multi-millionaire. Meanwhile Bud Ornstein resigned from UA and went to live in Spain.'

Beatlemania was about young girls adoring four young men. 'They were great guys and they were great times,' reflects Harry, who met them for the first time just prior to the premiere of *Hard Day's Night*. 'That night at the London Pavilion in Piccadilly Circus changed the face of London film premieres forever, with hundreds and thousands of fans queuing outside cinemas for hours on end in the hope of catching a glimpse of their heroes. The style of premieres also changed that night. Though the Beatles did wear dinner jackets there was a much more informal air to the evening. At the premiere of *Help!*, their second film, George Harrison admitted, "We would be much happier in jeans and T-shirts." At subsequent big occasions, the boys wore lounge suits and then became even more informal in their dress.'

One actor who has vivid memories of the Beatles is Victor Spinetti, who appeared with them in *Hard Day's Night* and *Help!* He was with the boys in their chauffeur-driven limo at the first premiere. 'As the limousine edged through the screaming fans outside the cinema,' he recalls in his recently published autobiography, 'John said, "Push Paul out first. He's the prettiest." When the door did in fact open, a girl reached in, grabbed George's hair and tore at it. Out in the crowd, pushing our way through, I noticed blood trickling down his forehead.'

The London Pavilion was host to all the Beatles' films, being the flagship cinema of United Artists. The historic building was built in 1859 and was first a music hall right in the centre of London's Piccadilly. In 1934, the building was converted into a cinema at a cost of £45,000 and opened with Alexander Korda's production of *The Private Life of Don Juan*. It closed in 1981, when United Artists crashed. All but the outside walls were demolished to house the current shopping mall. It was and remains a very important part of the Beatles' history, during their brief but hugely successful movie career.

Piccadilly Circus, where the London Pavilion was situated had never seen a night like it. On 6 July, 1964 more than 30,000 people crammed into the Circus for the premiere of *Hard Day's Night*. I had met the Beatles for the first time, prior to the premiere at their press reception

The Fab Four themselves,
having braved the crowds,
arrive in the theatre to greet
guests and the press

© REX FEATURES

BELOW
The first Royal Command
Film Performance in 1946
saw huge crowds greet King
George VI and Queen
Elizabeth. We thought it
could never be repeated. Not
only was it repeated here it
was repeated ten-fold. It
took the police half an hour
to clear a path for guests

I had never witnessed such
crowds and absolute hysteria
in the West End with people
fainting all over the place

© REX FEATURES

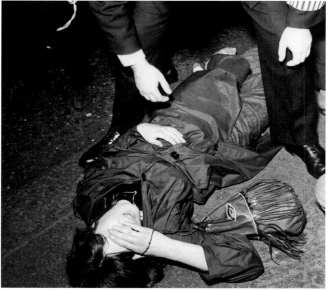

© REX FEATURES

Beatlemania was about young girls adoring four young men. They were all too willing to support the group through the vast merchandising campaign that built up around them, as illustrated by the three girls at a Variety Club function

BELOW
The Beatles had just arrived back from a mammoth tour of Australia, where fans had eclipsed those in the United States. Princess Margaret was guest of honour at the Royal World Premiere

Richard Lester, the American-born director who had been associated with the radio and TV 'Goon' shows, brought his own inimitable style to the Beatle films. Here he is pictured at the premiere with George Harrison and manager Brian Epstein

BELOW
In December 1961 Brian Epstein became the manager of the Fab Four until his untimely death in 1967. He is seen here at the premiere of *Hard Day's Night* with his protégés

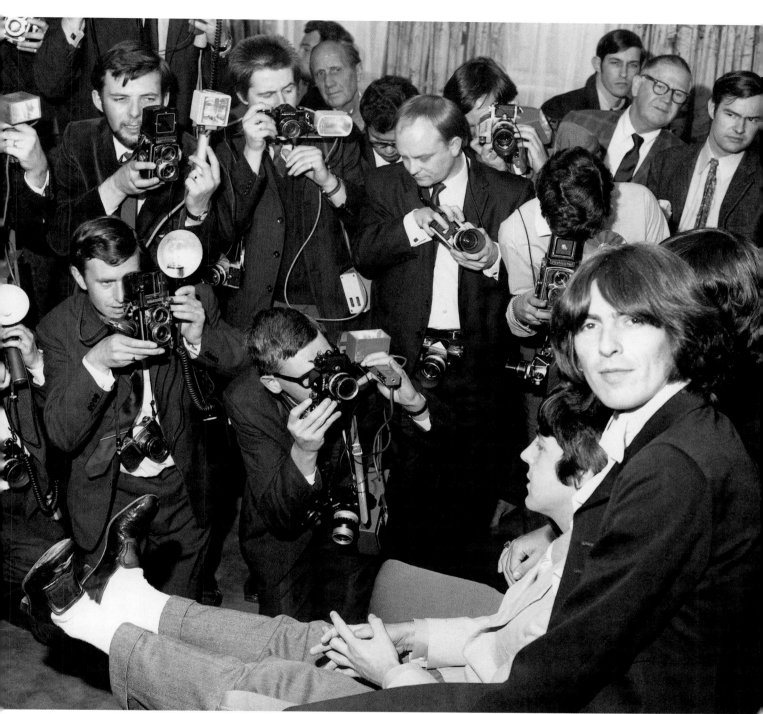

June 1968. The Beatles faced yet another battery of press cameras, this time to promote *Yellow Submarine*. It was the Beatles' first animated film, although apart from the soundtrack their contribution was minimal

When John Lennon was unable to make the press launch of *Yellow Submarine*, the boys produced a cartoon character of John

**BELOW**
Huge crowds the police encountered at their first film still followed the Beatles. This was the scene on 17 June 1968 when *Yellow Submarine* was premiered.

© REX FEATURES

© REX FEATURES

**ABOVE**

Mr and Mrs George Harrison, Mr and Mrs Ringo Starr, Yoko Ono and John Lennon and Paul McCartney take front row seats for *Yellow Submarine*. On the far left of picture is George Cole, before his success in TV's *Minder* series and in the second row at the London Pavilion is Keith Richards of the Rolling Stones

Front of House for *Yellow Submarine*. Again guests had to fight their way into the cinema

© REX FEATURES

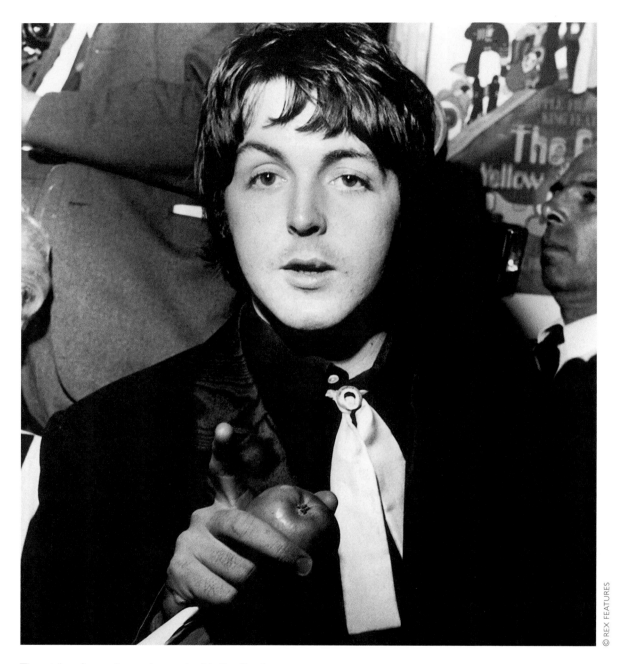

© REX FEATURES

The style of premieres changed with the Beatles. Previously premieres saw the stars turn out in wonderful gowns, adorned with tiaras and the men in full evening dress, resplendent with decorations and awards. Though the Beatles did wear dinner jackets for royal occasions, they brought a much more informal air to these events. Here is Paul McCartney at the *Yellow Submarine* premiere, holding an apple … the Beatles' record company was called Apple Corp!

OPPOSITE ▶
Cilla Black, another Liverpudlian, was a great friend of the group. She is seen here with George Harrison and Patti Boyd at the premiere of *Alfie*, for which she sang the title song

At the height of their togetherness, Paul McCartney and Jane Asher attend the premiere of *Alfie*

18 October 1967. A resplendent John Lennon at the premiere of *How I Won the War*. Brian Epstein had been found dead in bed in the August of that year. His funeral in Liverpool was a family affair and not attended by the Beatles. They attended his memorial service at the New London Synagogue in Abbey Road before going on to the premiere of *How I Won the War* the next day

George Harrison and his wife Patti Boyd at the *How I Won the War* premiere

**BELOW**

After the break-up of the Beatles, Ringo Starr carried on making films, one of which was *The Magic Christian* where he played Peter Sellers' son. At the end of filming party, 300 guests were invited to a gaming evening at Les Ambassadeurs, the popular West End restaurant and casino. Guests were given £1 million to play with on arrival, but the bills featured photos of Ringo and Peter Sellers!

This was the last photo I took of John Lennon. Here he's with Yoko Ono at the premiere of *The Magic Christian* campaigning for Britain to give peace a chance

OPPOSITE ▶
After divorcing from his wife Maureen in July 1975, six years later Ringo Starr wedded the lovely Barbara Bach, who had starred with Roger Moore in the James Bond epic *The Spy Who Loved Me*

Now man and wife after marrying in March, 1969, Paul and Linda McCartney attended the after premiere party for MGM's *That's Entertainment*

© REX FEATURES

© REX FEATURES

Post-premiere parties,
brought stars together for
evenings of fun. Here Ringo
Starr joins Mia Farrow on
the dance floor

# THREE

✦

# THE HOLLYWOOD ICONS

In 1913 legendary film maker Cecil B. DeMille was filming a cowboy picture in Flagstaff, Arizona.

Neither the location nor the climate was to his liking and he moved his production staff to a much more conducive suburb of Los Angeles. All the major studios followed, and the suburb known as Hollywood shortly became the centre of the motion picture business. The key creative talent, from studio leaders, producers, cameramen, writers, make-up artists, hairdressers, publicity personnel and the hangers-on all began to descend on America's west coast.

By the early 1900s, films had become a regular, staple diet of people's lives. Cinemas were being built in every village, town and city and by 1910 there were 9,480 cinemas in the USA. In 1914 there were 3,500 cinemas in the UK though 75 per cent of the programmes being screened were American films.

In 1913 William Fox formed a company that would become the mighty Twentieth Century Fox. The following year Paramount Pictures Corp was formed and just two years later the world's largest motion picture facility, Universal City Studios, opened its doors on a 230-acre converted farm, just beyond Hollywood. Hollywood fast became the centre of American – and thus the world – film production. Its domination had begun. Emerging were the movers and the shakers of the film epicentre – the icons: giants like Cecil B. DeMille, Sam Goldwyn, D.W. Griffith, Louis B. Mayer, the Warner Brothers, Harry Cohn of Columbia Pictures, David O. Selznick, Howard Hughes, Darryl Zanuck and Walt Disney.

Some of the film-makers became as famous as their stars. Moguls controlled the industry they had invented. They were master showmen with no fewer than 200 million people paying to see their product each week. During the Golden Days of Hollywood, the names in lights above their cinemas included Garbo, Dietrich, Gable, Astaire, Cooper, Grant, Niven, Chaplin, Bogart, Garland, Hepburn, Flynn, Tracy and Davis. Over time, Hollywood, through the emergence of television, was forced to change gear. New icons such as Stephen Spielberg. Martin Scorcese, Jerry Bruckheimer, George Lucas, the Weinstein brothers, Sherry Lansing, James Cameron and Jeffrey Katzenberg were handed the reins.

Though many studios are now controlled by accountants and committees, the moguls do still exist. But in recent years, it has been the stars who have adopted the role to a great extent. When, back in 1953, Lew Wasserman, then an agent but later to become boss of Universal, negotiated a deal on *Winchester '73* for James Stewart that saw the actor take a smaller fee for his role but a percentage of the profits, little did anyone think it would snowball and that the stars would become dictators with ever-increasing demands.

I photographed Jayne Mansfield talking to the legendary Cecil B. DeMille at the premiere of *Les Girls* in 1957. I didn't dare ask if Mr DeMille was ready for his close up!

OPPOSITE ▶
One of the greatest names in the British film industry was Lord (J. Arthur) Rank. Pictured here on the right, he is chatting to the managing director of his empire, The Rank Organisation, John Davis. Their respective wives, Lady Rank (*left*) and Dinah Sheridan are also enjoying a chat

ABOVE

The Queen, accompanied by Princess Margaret at the premiere of *Battle of the River Plate*, meets Emeric Pressberger and (just to his right) Michael Powell. Together they were 'The Archers' and made some terrific, and some of the best, British films. This was one of them

Roll on a few decades and my son Scott met Walt's nephew, Roy Disney. He arrived in London with his wife Patricia for the special millennium IMAX re-issue of *Fantasia*

◀ OPPOSITE

Walt Disney was embarking upon a programme of films in the UK with such titles as *Treasure Island*, *The Sword and the Rose*, *Rob Roy*, *In Search of the Castaways*, *The Moonspinners* and so forth. He planned on making a rare trip over, and the publicity department was charged with getting as much mileage out of his trip as possible. I had to go up to the Dorchester to meet Disney's publicity director, Arthur Allighan, who had recently been appointed to the new Disney HQ in London. I went up to Walt's suite, which was directly above the main door canopy, and which he liked very much. The idea was mooted of taking Walt and his wife down to Disney Street and Disney Place one Sunday morning to shoot some photos for use in the UK and US press. Little did the residents know who this great man was, standing on the corner of their streets

It was at the Royal Premiere of *To Catch a Thief* in 1955 that I again met Alfred Hitchcock, pictured here arriving with his wife Alma. I say again because a couple of years earlier I had been called in to Madame Tussaud's wax museum to photograph the famous director next to his effigy. Sadly that photograph was for an agency that no longer exists, and was trashed when their offices were closed. At the premiere Hitch was, as always, very gracious and rather excited that his film was selected for the Royal Film Performance. That very evening I recall it was announced that Princess Margaret was not going to marry Peter Townsend, so it was quite memorable for a couple of reasons. By that time, Hitch was a US citizen and spent little time in England. When he returned to these shores to direct *Frenzy* in 1972, it caused quite a stir with the UK press and I was called in to help launch the film. The idea was that Hitch would turn up at the Plaza cinema, climb onto a cherry picker and place the last letter 'Y' on the front of the huge billboard to spell FRENZY. Wow, I thought, what a shot that would be. Hitch duly arrived, looked at the cherry picker and declined! So all of my shots are of him outside the cinema with the smaller billboards.

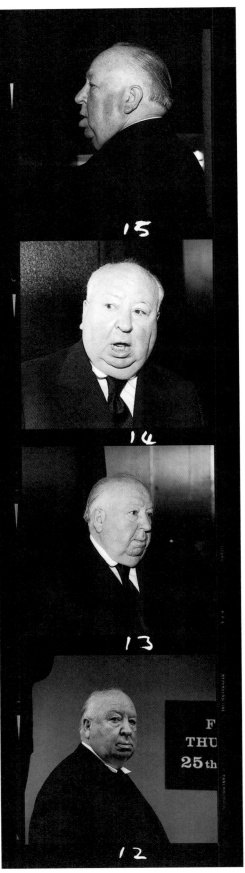

Toots Bounds, Gary Cooper and Adolph Zukor at the premiere of *Rob Roy*. From beginning his career with penny arcades, offering moving peepshows that evolved into nickelodeon theatres, Zukor made short films and then features. He eventually consolidated several smaller companies into what we know today as Paramount Pictures Corporation. He remained chairman until his death at the age of 103

Mike Frankovich, Judy Garland, Capucine and Otto Preminger at the premiere of *Song Without End* in 1960. Mike was a great friend of mine, he was managing director of Columbia Pictures as well as being a producer in his own right

It's more than a movie.
It's a celebration.

Here is Mr Preminger again, pictured at the premiere of *That's Entertainment II* in 1976. Though a distinguished film-maker, I have to say that he wasn't a liked man in the business. Though I never had any dealings with him, a great friend of mine who became publicity director at Paramount was fired after Preminger, who was filming a Paramount picture in London, complained to the board that their director of publicity had not been to see him, and pay homage. He insisted my friend be fired. It looks as though I could be asking him about the incident here

© REX FEATURES

Legendary producers Cubby
Broccoli and Sam Spielgel
meet at the post-premiere
party of *Lawrence of Arabia*. I
had met Sam on a number of
occasions, and was delighted,
when on holiday, my wife and
I visited a restaurant in San
Remo and saw Sam there. He
leapt up and greeted me like
a long lost friend

© REX FEATURES

Two other creative masters,
David Lean and Freddie
Young, the director and
director of photography on
*Lawrence of Arabia*

© REX FEATURES

© REX FEATURES

**ABOVE**

In 1978 the Royal Film Performance was to be a science fiction film called *Close Encounters of the Third Kind*. It was directed by an up-and-coming young American called Steven Spielberg. We didn't know too much about him, but he's done rather well since!

Roll on a few years, and here is a slightly older Steven Spielberg in London again, though this time with his mother, Leah Adler

Richard Zanuck cuts the haggis at the post party premiere of *The Prime of Miss Jean Brodie* at Claridges. He was then president of Twentieth Century Fox, the company which financed the film

My son Scott caught up with
Richard Zanuck thirty years
later, here with Eric Clapton,
at a London charity event.
Zanuck has gone on to
produce some of the biggest
hit films of the intervening
decades — *Jaws*, *Cocoon*,
*Driving Miss Daisy*, *Charlie and
the Chocolate Factory* and his
latest, *Sweeney Todd*

© REX FEATURES

BELOW
Famed Italian producer
Dino De Laurentis joins
Michael Winner for a
cigar at the premiere of
*Moonraker* in 1979

© REX FEATURES

The Charleston champion and TV mogul Lord (Lew) Grade takes the floor with Nanette Newman, at the party following the premiere of *A Chorus Line*

Not to be outdone, Lew Grade's brother, Lord (Bernard) Delfont with Lady Cave shows that he too can trip the light fantastic. Lord Delfont was head of EMI films

Fred Zinneman enjoys a
drink with Romy Schneider
at Claridges following the
premiere of *Lord Jim* in 1965

The wonderful Sophia Loren, here with her husband Carlo Ponti – the producer of hit films such as *Dr Zhivago*, *Blowup* and around 150 Italian movies. They married twice, and remained so until his death in 2007

**BELOW**
Scott went along to the post premiere party of *Star Wars Episode I*. Here are Laurence Fishburne, director George Lucas, Ewan McGregor and Natalie Portman. It did rather well, taking some $925 million world wide

◄ **OPPOSITE**
American director John Huston made the wonderful family film *Annie* in 1982. I remember that they held the auditions for the lead girl at the Dorchester Hotel and I was asked to go along to take photos. I was there all day, and for weeks afterwards all I could hear in my head was the song 'Tomorrow, tomorrow....' The part eventually went to Aileen Quinn, pictured here with Huston

**BELOW**
Hugh Hudson and David Puttnam, now Lord Puttnam, were the director-producer team on *Chariots of Fire* which went on to scoop the best picture Oscar

**ABOVE**
Charles Bluhdorn and Franco Zeffirelli share a conversation at the premiere of *Romeo and Juliet* in 1968. Mr Bluhdorn was president of Gulf & Western which took over Paramount Pictures. Shortly after the takeover he arrived in London and arranged a visit to their prime cinema in the UK, the Plaza on Lower Regent Street in London. The manager was an old friend of mine, Max Gayton, and he asked me to go along and photograph Bludhorn. He was most impressed with the beautiful cinema, with antique furniture, paintings and carpets. 'Mr Gayton,' he said ' this is a marvellous theatre. I have not seen anything like it before. Don't let anyone alter a thing!' Within two years the cinema was split into two screens

◀ **OPPOSITE**
The wonderful Richard Attenborough, now Lord Attenborough, with his wife of sixty-two years, Sheila Sim, attends the premiere of *Chaplin*

Roman Polanski with Sharon Tate, his wife of just over a year. She, and four others, were murdered by members of the Manson family in 1969. She was pregnant at the time

One of the heads of the UK's most successful production company Working Title, Tim Bevan, with his then wife Joely Richardson, attends the premiere of his film *French Kiss* in 1995

Mike Todd Jr dances
with Elizabeth Taylor

John Schlesinger, director of
such notable films as *Billy
Liar*, *Midnight Cowboy* and
*Marathon Man*, attends the
premiere of *Empire of the Sun*
accompanied by his mother

**ABOVE**

Modern day moguls. The Weinstein brothers, Harvey and Bob, flank director Robert Rodriguez at the premiere of *Sin City*. The Weinsteins have been involved with green-lighting almost two hundred films. From them there have been sixty-five BAFTA awards, seventy-five Oscars, with their company Miramax holding a library and assets worth $2 billion, and making millions in profit for their parent company Disney. However, Harvey Weinstein said 'all that and Michael Eisner [Disney's CEO] still won't renew our contract'. It led to the brothers forming their independent The Weinstein Company in 2004

Jerry Bruckheimer attends the London premiere of *Pearl Harbor* with one of its stars, Kate Beckinsale, in 2001

© REX FEATURES

Oliver Stone, Al Pacino and Jamie Foxx arrive for the premiere of their film *Any Given Sunday* at the Warner Bros. theatre in Leicester Square in 1999

**BELOW**

Alan Ladd Jr being presented to Princess Margaret at the premiere of *Silver Streak* in 1977. Ladd was President of Twentieth Century Fox which produced this movie. Under his tenure *Star Wars*, *Alien* and *Young Frankenstein*, were a few of the classics green lit. In 1979 Ladd left his position as President at Fox to found his own production company, The Ladd Company. He enjoyed great successes with comedies like *Night Shift* and *Police Academy* and Oscar winners *The Right Stuff* and Best Picture, *Chariots of Fire*. In 1985, Ladd joined MGM/UA, eventually becoming Chairman and CEO of Pathe Entertainment. During his time, MGM/UA enjoyed hits like *A Fish Called Wanda*, *Moonstruck*, and *Thelma & Louise*. Ladd reformed The Ladd Company with Paramount Pictures in 1993 where he produced the hits *The Brady Bunch* and Best Picture winner *Braveheart*

© REX FEATURES

The Royal Film Performance 1974. *The Three Musketeers.*
Producer Alexander Salkind is being presented to the Queen
Mother. Salkind was famous for shooting two movies at once.
Sequels would appear fast on the heels on the first film! In
1975 *The Four Musketeers* hit British screens

© REX FEATURES

# FOUR

# THE LEADING PLAYERS:
## Those Were the Days

'Acting talent is not enough. A star must possess another mysterious quality, which you might call personality, magnetism, glamour.

The essence of it is the capacity to stir the imagination of the audience, to make them feel that there is much more to the actor or actress than meets the eye and ear.' Thus American director Rouben Mamoulian described stardom back in the 1960s. It still stands good today. And Harry Myers' camera attracted the personalities to his camera, like bees to luscious blossom.

Back in the early days of the cinema some hundred years ago, actors and actresses were paid modest fees, like any other job. Until then the only 'celebrities' were the likes of presidents, monarchs, war heroes, politicians, writers and criminals. Whilst there had been some familiar faces, until this time, no one actually knew who *they* were!

By the early 1900s, cinema was becoming the main form of entertainment and it then became the norm to credit the actors in films. The emergence of the star system in the US can be traced back to a single event, focusing on the controversial move of the actress Florence Lawrence from Biograph to the Independent Motion Picture Company in 1910. This shift, accompanied by 'the first publicity stunt on behalf of a motion picture star', is seen to signify 'the beginning of the star system'.

The publicity was all due to producer Carl Laemmle, the founder of Universal Pictures. He circulated a rumour that the 'Biograph girl', whom he now revealed to be Florence Lawrence, had been killed in a car crash. The statement was made simply to boost sales figures for Lawrence's forthcoming film, and was denied in a press release, which provided further publicity. From that point it was realized how important the stars of a film could be for attracting greater audiences.

Soon, film stars became household names: Mary Pickford, Lillian Gish, Douglas Fairbanks, Rudolph Valentino and the most famous of them all, Charlie Chaplin. The phenomenal success of stars such as Charlie Chaplin and Mary Pickford, who were to go on to form their own film production company United Artists, showed the studios the benefits of marketing their performers strongly.

Through the 1920s, 1930s and 1940s, stars were tied by contract to a particular studio (such as MGM, Twentieth Century Fox or Paramount), who were responsible for the branding of the stars' images, and the marketing of products related to them. Fan magazines became particularly popular during this period. They were often simply an excuse to carry gossip to promote the stars' film activities, their love lives and fashion choices.

The importance of the star system has continued through to the present day. During the Second World War Britons craved their staple diet of Hollywood films, becoming regular cinemagoers. From 1946 the Hollywood tsars saw that not only were big budget American films made in Britain with a guaranteed box-office result but also that their leading players had a high profile at film premieres and publicity tours.

Many films are successful solely because they are vehicles for famous actors and actresses. The Hollywood studio system may have declined to a certain extent but it and powerful independent producers who maintain the lifestyle and looks of stars are usually as important in building their image as the strength of their acting. Their lives are heavily scrutinized by the media. Generally most publicity is seen to be good for raising their and their current film's profile. Stars whose appeal is aimed at the teen and young adult market are particularly carefully groomed to provide the right image for their fans.

Though there are in excess of a hundred premieres in London annually, each is awaited and greeted with great anticipation. Now have a glimpse of the heroes and heroines of the leading players from Hollywood, Europe and Britain that Harry Myers has focused on in a career spanning more than sixty years.

© REX FEATURES

© REX FEATURES

I took the first photo of Kim Novak at the after-premiere party of *Once More with Feeling* on 31 March 1960. The second photograph was taken by my son Scott on 13 May 1997 at the opening of a new multiplex cinema in Newham. Back in 1960, I had the pleasure of going to meet her at Dover. She came over from the US by boat, and I photographed her arriving, getting on the train and so forth. I realized that I had to dash up to Blackpool for the CEA (Cinema Exhibitors Association) conference, followed by a big party thrown by Columbia, so made my getaway … only to discover who the conference's special guest was – Kim Novak. She was lovely, and insisted that we have a dance together. So a morning assignment in Dover turned into a very pleasant dance in Blackpool

American star James Garner and his wife Lois Clarke share a funny story with Richard Attenborough and his wife, Sheila Sim, at the Royal premiere of Garner's film *Move Over Darling* in 1964

A modern day star, Kate Winslet, here accompanied by her brother Joss Sibling at the premiere of her film *Iris* in 2002 at the Curzon Mayfair. She was the first actress to be nominated for four Oscars before turning 30. Her fifth nomination in 2007 was for *Little Children*

Albert Finney and Shirley Anne Field at the post-premiere party of *Lawrence of Arabia* – a film he turned down the lead role in, and which in turn made a star of Peter O'Toole

© REX FEATURES

Continuing with the dancing theme, here is Shirley MacLaine dancing the night away at Claridges

© REX FEATURES

Back in 1953 Paramount asked me to look after Montgomery Clift, who was then a huge star and in London for a royal premiere. They didn't just want me to photograph him, but to stay with him at the Savoy Hotel and show him around London. 'Harry, you know what I really want to do?' he asked me one day. 'I want to ride on top of a bus and I want to meet the real people of London.' I suggested if he wanted to meet real people there were none better than my family. My parents thought I was joking when I told them that Montgomery Clift would be coming home for lunch. We lived in Euston back then, in a flat on the fourth floor. So Montgomery and I hopped on a bus outside the Savoy and up to the top deck we climbed. There he sat, feet stretched out, loving every minute. My mother was thrilled when we arrived. She had done a Sunday lunch – roast beef, Yorkshire pudding and all the trimmings. But you know, I never took a photograph! How embarrassing of me to admit. After Monty returned home to the USA I received a call from a Paramount executive. 'I've got a big parcel for you. You'd better come up and collect it.' It was from Monty. It was a massive side of beef for my mother, with gratitude! Here he is dancing with Linda Christian at the Savoy hotel, James Stewart is in the background

Can't act; slightly bald; can dance a little. That was the studio report on the first screen test Fred Astaire undertook. Here he is arriving in London for the gala screening of *That's Entertainment II* in 1976

BELOW
No fewer than sixty-eight British and American stars assembled for the premiere of the MGM musical, *Because You're Mine*, in 1952. One of them was the great Gene Kelly. Here he signs an autograph for a fan, Susan Potts

Roll on twenty-five years and here is Gene Kelly again. Liza Minelli accepts his invitation to the dance

© REX FEATURES

© REX FEATURES

**HERE AND OPPOSITE ▶**
Cairo Fred (aka Omar Shariff) and Lawrence (aka Peter O'Toole) provide the after show party entertainment following the Royal premiere of *Lawrence of Arabia*. Noel Coward was to add his own postscript: 'If Peter had been any prettier it should have been called Florence of Arabia'

Tony Curtis, in town filming *The Persuaders!* in 1971, took time out to join in a post-premiere party at the Savoy with his wife Lesley Allen

OPPOSITE ▶

John Wayne arrives in London in 1964 to film *Circus World* at Pinewood Studios. Stepping off the plane, minus his hairpiece, he is greeted by Paramount's Tony Redding, their head of publicity

OPPOSITE ▶

Here he is again, the Duke, this time with his hairpiece. He is dancing with Constance Smith at the Savoy

**BELOW**
Back to dancing again. This terrific shot of Johnny Weissmuller and his wife dancing is one of my favourites; he was a giant of a man and, of course, most famous for playing Tarzan. At the *That's Entertainment II* party, at the Dorchester, he impressed us all by tripping the light fantastic with his wife

The delightful Kay Kendall and Kenneth More take to the floor at the *Rob Roy* premiere party in 1953. Kay sadly died a few years later from leukaemia. A great loss. Looking on here is actor Jack Hawkins

© REX FEATURES

◀ OPPOSITE

Tripping the light fantastic with Elizabeth Taylor is none other than acclaimed ballet dancer Rudolph Nureyev. Although I photographed her on several occasions, I shall never forget my first encounter with Elizabeth Taylor. It was, I think, around mid-1956 when I had a call to rush up to the Dorchester one day, from Columbia's head publicity man in London Alan Tucker. Elizabeth Taylor was staying there with her second husband Michael Wilding who was promoting a film called *Zarak*. When I got to the room Alan was talking with Michael Wilding, but there was no sign of Miss Taylor. 'Elizabeth and Michael need some passport-sized photos taken for a visa' said Alan 'and I thought you could do it.' Oh, I thought, OK. So I duly photographed Michael using my

5 × 4 Speed Graphic camera which, being rather large, is certainly not the ideal tool for the job. He then invited me to sit down, to wait for Elizabeth Taylor to ready herself, and we had a little chat but I could see he was getting anxious that his wife hadn't appeared. 'Are you ready darling?' he called out. 'The photographer is here.' She appeared from the bedroom, wearing a black see-through negligee. You could certainly see everything! I picked up my camera and asked myself if I dare step back to do a full length shot as opposed to just head and shoulders – with it being quite a large camera I'd have needed to step back a good few paces. As Michael Wilding and Alan were watching me intently, I thought I'd better not! Imagine how much that photograph would have been worth

I just love this photograph of Peter Finch, who we all knew as Finchy. He was one of the great characters of the film business, and ever the practical joker. This was in 1973 at a party held at Les Ambassadeurs, following the Royal Film Performance of *Lost Horizon*. He's dancing with Jill St Amant

© REX FEATURES

Kirk Douglas and Peggy Cummins pause for a photograph at the party following the royal premiere of *Because You're Mine*

© REX FEATURES

© REX FEATURES

Here's an early shot of Jackie Collins from 1955, long before she became a best-selling author, at the Odeon Marble Arch. The film premiere was *Footsteps in the Fog*

Here is Jackie's sister, Joan Collins. I first met Joan in the early 1950s when she was under contract to Rank. I was then working in Fleet Street, and she came down to our studio one day for a session of studio photographs. We built a set with sand and desert island type backings. She brought quite a few changes of clothes with her, and took the dressing room that was adjacent to the dark room. She'll probably kill me for revealing this, but I found out that the boys in the darkroom had drilled peep holes through the wall and watched with great excitement as she changed!

© REX FEATURES

© REX FEATURES

◄ OPPOSITE AND THIS PAGE

Having seen her debut performance in *Tiger Bay* (1959) Walt Disney offered Hayley Mills a five-year contract. She was poised to head to the US to become an international sensation as Pollyanna, and win a special Oscar. However, ahead of the movie starting, Walt was keen to get a series of publicity photos taken of Hayley. His UK press officer John Willis called me up and asked if I'd be able to spend a day at the Millses' farmhouse in Kent with him to take some photos of Hayley and the family – Walt was very keen to push the family angle. John, Mary and Jonathan are seen here with Hayley. Her sister Juliet was, at that time, away at stage school. Hayley was an absolute joy to work with, and despite her tender years, was very much grounded and unspoilt. Incidentally, one of my shots made the front cover of *LIFE* magazine

© REX FEATURES

The premiere of the second film compilation of highlights from the MGM film library was hosted by Fred Astaire and Gene Kelly. It literally featured a who's who in terms of cast list: Judy Garland, Mickey Rooney, Bing Crosby, Greer Garson, Clark Gable, Nelson Eddy, Doris Day, Jimmy Durante, Joan Crawford, Elizabeth Taylor, Ronald Colman, W.C. Fields and countless others. Its London premiere was in 1976 at the Empire Leicester Square. The turn-out was fantastic. Jack Hayley Jr spared no expense in flying the stars in, and I was there to photograph them. On stage at the Empire, Gene Kelly introduced a host of stars in attendance: Fred Astaire, Kathryn Grayson, Leslie Caron, Johnny Weissmuller, Donald O'Connor, along with producers and studio executives. Gene Kelly captivated the audience with tales of the golden days of Hollywood before introducing the film

© REX FEATURES

© REX FEATURES

© REX FEATURES

**ABOVE LEFT**

A candid shot of Dirk Bogarde and Judy Garland. They starred together in Garland's last film, *I Could Go on Singing*, which filmed at Shepperton Studios in 1962. It wasn't an easy film, not least due to Miss Garland. On the last day of shooting when the director called it a wrap, Judy Garland looked at the crew and said, 'You'll miss me when I've gone'. She was right. We do

**ABOVE RIGHT**

The delightful Dame Edith Evans at the premiere of *The Slipper and the Rose* in 1976 which was directed by Bryan Forbes, who is kneeling next to her. Gemma Craven is on her other side

Joseph Cotton is accompanied by his wife Patricia Medina

© REX FEATURES

Henry Fonda arrives at a premiere at London's Columbia Theatre. His career spanned almost fifty years. He finally won the Best Actor Academy Award in 1982, the year of his death, for Lord Grade's most acclaimed film *On Golden Pond*

Archie Leach, or as we knew him, Cary Grant, arriving at the *Once More with Feeling* premiere. I'd met him before actually, at a cinema manager's conference, where he was the special guest. My wife, Anne, accompanied me as she was a great fan. After a short while of meeting and greeting, his publicity man said that they had to go off to another engagement, though just as he reached the door, Cary Grant looked back and saw Anne standing near the bar, smiling. He walked back in and said, 'You are the one person I haven't met that I would like to.' It made Anne's year!

© REX FEATURES

Momma Dearest. One of
Hollywood's most endurable
actresses, Joan Crawford,
in 1966. She had a bit of
a reputation … and lived
up to it!

Jane Russell and Anna Neagle. RKO pictures had flown Miss Russell over to the UK to promote one of their films and she was staying in a suite at the Savoy Hotel. The studio's publicist, David Jones, asked me to go up to the hotel and stay all day to photograph her with the various people that would be seeing her – from members of the press, to friends and celebrities. I duly arrived about 9.30 a.m., and went up to the suite. David greeted me and said Miss Russell was in the bedroom, changing and wasn't yet ready, so we sat down for a chat in the lounge whilst we waited. A voice boomed out from the bedroom, 'David I don't know what I should wear. What should I wear?' David replied, 'Well what have you got?' With that Jane Russell walked into the lounge from her bedroom, without a stitch on, holding a couple of outfits. David nearly fell off his chair, whilst I instinctively reached down for my camera – though it was just out of reach on this occasion! Totally unfazed, Miss Russell asked David's advice as to which she should wear and trotted back into the bedroom. On another occasion, through David Jones, I was invited to the Café de Paris along with Jane

© REX FEATURES

Russell, who was going to meet Marlene Dietrich there. We sat down to eat and in came an *Evening Standard* reporter from the 'In London Last Night' column which, incidentally, was where Michael Winner started his career, along with a photographer – a little man of about 4' 11'' by the name of Bill Breeze. Bill had seen me dance with Jane Russell and not quite realizing I was actually a guest of hers and David's, decided he'd chance his arm and ask her to dance too. I think it'd be fair to say that he'd been to several parties

beforehand, and consumed a reasonable amount of alcohol, and in taking Jane on to the dance floor we could see he only came up to her chest. Just then, he plunged his head right into her breast and shook his head whilst blowing air out through his closed lips quite noisily. David Jones was furious and had Bill kicked out, and wrote to the editor of the Standard saying how ashamed he was that his guest should be treated in such a manner by his photographer. Bill Breeze got the sack!

Alan Ladd and his wife Sue Carrol at the *Because You're Mine* premiere in 1952. They were in London filming *The Black Knight*. Ladd was a hugely popular star, though his career was controlled very much by his wife. Cubby Broccoli, producer of *The Black Knight*, realized halfway through the shoot that re-writes were called for, to make sense of an ever-changing story, and the job fell to Bryan Forbes. He had to link footage in the can with the rest of the script – the two halves just did not sit happily together. Sue Ladd had script approval – that was in the contract. Every word uttered by Ladd had first to be approved by her. Forbes came up with some pages in which Ladd dodged a few arrows, vaulted from the castle battlements into a cart of hay, sliced a few of the villains in two with his sword, seized a horse and galloped across the rising drawbridge just in time. What was Mrs Ladd's verdict? 'Alan Ladd does not steal horses.' She went on to explain that if he did they would lose the Boy Scouts Association, the Daughters of the American Revolution and probably half his fan club. Everyone was dumbfounded. However, Irving Allen, Cubby's partner, said, 'Sue, he's not stealing a horse, he's borrowing one.' She was not convinced. So Bryan Forbes came up with a line, when Ladd has done his vaulting and slicing, that he would deliver to a sentry, 'Is this the horse I ordered?' He jumps onto it and gallops off. Sue agreed it! And that's what they shot

ABOVE
Two masters of the funny ditty: Noel Coward with Joyce Grenfell

ABOVE RIGHT
Robert Morley, resplendent in full evening attire, arrives at the premiere of *Lord Jim* at the Odeon Leicester Square (now re-christened the Odeon West End) on 15 February 1965

© REX FEATURES

Michael and Shakira Caine attend the premiere of *The Fourth Protocol* in 1987. He has since become a Knight of the British Empire and his official title is Sir Michael Caine CBE. Quite a lot of people know that. In the days when Lady Caine was still a model, before she married Michael, one of my assignments was to photograph her at the Ideal Home Show in Earl's Court

◄ OPPOSITE
Richard Burton chats with Italian star Gina Lollobrigida at *The Taming of the Shrew* on 27 February 1967. This was the first of two Shakespearean works to be directed by Franco Zefferelli. The following year came *Romeo and Juliet*. Unfortunately, the Queen Mother had to withdraw from the premiere of *Shrew* on medical advice and Princess Margaret headed the Royal party

Jerry Lewis, in town filming
*Don't Raise the Bridge, Lower
the River* was one of the
invited guests at the *You Only
Live Twice* premiere in 1967

RIGHT
**Rex Harrison escorts Vivien
Leigh to the Odeon
Leicester Square**

**OPPOSITE ▶**
Bob Hope and the beautiful Audrey Hepburn pictured together in
1961. I first met Audrey in 1950. I used to go to a club called Ciro's and
photograph the personalities for the various socialite magazines like Tatler.
During one of my visits, a charming couple named Leonard and Jackie
Urry invited me to sit down for drinks. Leonard was an impresario and
he'd put on floor shows there, where one of the performers was Audrey
Hepburn. She was so beautiful. We got on very well, and enjoyed a few
dinners and dances before she was spotted by the Associated British
Picture Corporation's Bob Leonard and signed to a film contract for
*Laughter in Paradise*. Shortly after, Paramount spotted her in an ABPC film
and offered her a contract in Hollywood for *Roman Holiday* with Gregory
Peck. Ah, what might have been!

With her beauty often compared to that of Audrey Hepburn, British star Keira Knightley is fast becoming one of the world's biggest stars. She was 21 when Scott took this photo of her in 2006 at the *Pirates of the Caribbean 2* premiere in London. Her big hit came in 2002 with *Bend It Like Beckham* since when she has made an impressive fifteen films

I don't think Dustin Hoffman is ever particularly comfortable being the centre of attention, but when *Kramer vs Kramer* was chosen for the Royal Film of 1980, he had little choice. Here he is with Merryl Streep and Justin Henry in the balcony lounge of the Odeon Leicester Square. Young Justin and Hoffman worked extremely well together on screen and I know that prior to each scene the pair discussed at length what they would do and how they would approach it. Interestingly, the main parts were first offered to Jane Fonda and James Caan who both turned them down

Here he is again, getting a motherly cuddle from Dame Vera Lynn at the post-premiere party, which was at The White Elephant on the River. Dustin Hoffman played the drums at the party. Very good he was too

© REX FEATURES

My son Scott took this terrific photo of the Harry Potter children. This was at the premiere of their first film *Harry Potter and the Philosopher's Stone* and shows, from left to right, Rupert Grint, Daniel Radcliffe and Emma Watson

OPPOSITE ▶

Although she was a child star in the USA, Jodie Foster wasn't that well known in Britain. I was asked if I would take a series of shots of her, at famous London landmarks such as Big Ben, Trafalgar Square and Piccadilly Circus, for the studio behind *Bugsy Malone*. A delightful young lady who has gone on to great things. Incidentally, she was the first choice to play Princess Leia in *Star Wars* but a contract with Walt Disney prevented her taking the role

A line-up of stars. Dana Andrews, Joan Crawford and Victor Mature arrive for the 1956 premiere of *Battle of the River Plate*

© REX FEATURES

Deborah Kerr pictured with her writer husband Peter Viertel. Viertel worked closely with John Huston, particularly on *The African Queen*. He later wrote a script entitled *White Hunter Black Heart* – the film of which starred Clint Eastwood in 1990. It was a thinly veiled account of his time with Huston on *The African Queen*

© REX FEATURES

A powerhouse couple in Hollywood and both Oscar winners. Michael Douglas, who produced the Academy award success *One Flew Over the Cuckoo's Nest*, with his Welsh-born wife Catherine Zeta Jones. She won best actress Oscar for *Chicago*.

© REX FEATURES

The Governor of California (aka Arnold Schwarzenegger). A former Mr Universe, Arnie came to fame in the era of the big blockbuster Holly-wood movies

© REX FEATURES

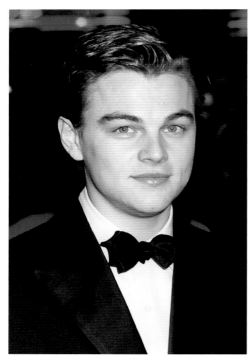

© REX FEATURES

A young Leonardo DiCaprio
arrives for the Royal
premiere of *Titanic*, which at
195 minutes was the longest
film the Royal party had to
sit through. Leonardo's love
affair with Kate Winslet in
the Oscar-winning film raised
him to super stardom

Sandra Bullock enchants the
Leicester Square crowd at
the premiere of *Miss
Congeniality* which she also
produced

© REX FEATURES

The queen of pop, Madonna, and her co-star Rupert Everett arrive for a rather casual premiere of *The Next Best Thing*

*Forrest Gump* and *Philadelphia* won best actor Oscars in successive years for Tom Hanks – a feat only previously achieved by Spencer Tracy. But it was in his capacity as a producer that he is pictured here in 1996 with Liv Tyler, who starred in *That Thing You Do*

© REX FEATURES

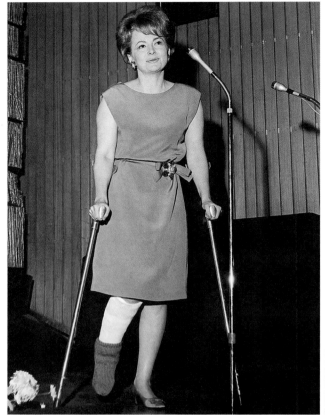

© REX FEATURES

ABOVE
James Caan gives the thumbs up at the premiere of *Funny Lady* in 1975, accompanied by Connie Kreski. Caan proved himself a bit of a trouble-maker on set at times; a fervent rodeo fan with the nickname 'The Jewish Cowboy', the actor snuck off during production to be in a roping competition in nearby Palm Springs. He returned with a broken thumb that had to be placed in a cast; director Herb Ross engineered inventive ways to film around it

© REX FEATURES

ABOVE
Another plaster cast! Olivia de Havilland arrives on stage at the National Film Theatre on 5 November 1965 with a broken leg

Olivia de Havilland's sister, Joan Fontaine, also in town at the time, attended the premiere of *The Nanny* starring Bette Davis

© REX FEATURES

Being John Malkovich means you get to play opposite some of the world's top actresses. Here he is with Glenn Close at the *Dangerous Liaisons* party, following the premiere, at the Ivy

© REX FEATURES

A dapper Yul Brynner, no stranger to London premieres and first nights. Yul shaved his head for the Broadway production of *The King and I* and remained hairless ever after

Lee Remick at the premiere of *Funny Lady* in the presence of the Queen on 17 March 1975. She was in town filming *The Omen*

BELOW
James Mason, Sir Michael Redgrave, Rachel Kempson and star Lynn Redgrave at the premiere of *Georgy Girl* on 12 October 1966. *Georgy Girl* was one of the pictures which came out of Britain in the early sixties to lead the 'Swinging Sixties' scene

© REX FEATURES

© REX FEATURES

After the premiere of *Lord Jim* on 15 February 1965, a party was held at Claridges. It attracted a host of stars, including Jean Simmons and Laurence Harvey

© REX FEATURES

Angelica Huston. The daughter of eminent director John Huston was to grow into a star in her own right

© REX FEATURES

© REX FEATURES

He's not sticking his tongue out at Prince Charles. Mel Gibson is just showing the Prince how it was to be *The Man without a Face*. The sideburns were for Mel Gibson's character in *Maverick* which he had just started filming

The Mayfair Hotel was the venue following the premiere of *The Vikings*. Smoking was still the rage as Burt Lancaster and his companion Luciana Bouchi puffed away

One of the great stars of the West End musical theatre after the war, Dolores Gray was deep in conversation with Laurence Olivier after a ball at the Lyceum in Hammersmith

© REX FEATURES

John Gielgud was always one of Britain's greatest thespians. But it was Hollywood that turned him into an Oscar-winning star, thanks to his portrayal as Dudley Moore's worldly-wise butler in *Arthur*

The rockers. Mick Jagger and Marianne Faithful managed to get invitations to the premiere of Stanley Kubrick's *2001: A Space Odyssey*

**ABOVE**
More rockers. Often at first nights, Keith Richards of the Rolling Stones rolled up. Here he is at the premiere of the Beatles' animated effort, *Yellow Submarine*, in July 1968

Later to become the keeper of the Stones archives and also the leader of a jazz group and restaurateur, Bill Wyman was another of the Stones to attend *Yellow Submarine*

**OPPOSITE ▶**
Rank's *Battle of the River Plate* was chosen as the Royal Command film at the Empire, Leicester Square. French beauty, Brigitte Bardot, had been tempted to Pinewood to star in one of the very successful Doctor series. Here she is pictured with Rank starlets Maureen Swanson (later to become Countess of Dudley) and Belinda Lee, who was tragically killed in a road accident

A star from the early sixties in *If* and *Clockwork Orange*, Malcolm McDowell is pictured here by my son Scott at the premiere of *Master and Commander*, with one of the film's stars, Paul Bettany

Tom Cruise didn't have high heels on in this shot so his then wife, Nicole Kidman towers over him. They are pictured at the premiere of Stanley Kubrick's *Eyes Wide Shut* which, unfortunately, was to mark the end of their marriage

© REX FEATURES

© REX FEATURES

They were a forceful team in *Captain Corelli's Mandolin*. Nicholas Cage and Penelope Cruz on the red carpet for the first screening of the film in London

One of Britain's most successful and hard-working actors, Ewan McGregor, took the lead in *Rogue Trader*, alongside Anna Friel

© REX FEATURES

2007 has brought plaudits galore for Dame Helen Mirren. She has garnered awards from both side of the Atlantic. Not in her shadow but a massive figure in his own right is Helen's husband, director Taylor Hackford

© REX FEATURES

The Columbia picture *Cowboy*, starring Glenn Ford, received
its London premiere in 1958, and I'll always remember it
because to gain entry to the party afterwards the guests
had to dress up in western dress, including myself I might
add. There was the most wonderful party at the Pigalle in
Piccadilly and the film company brought over from Texas a
long 30-foot bar as well as these huge T-bone steaks. Whilst
I was inside photographing folks, including as we see here
English actors Tony Hancock and Sid James, we were all
called up to see Terry Thomas's entry. He'd ridden along
Piccadilly on horseback, dressed in his own anglicized
cowboy outfit, and brought the horse right the way in

© REX FEATURES

The night she became famous. Liz Hurley is pictured in the breathtaking, black Versace 'safety pin' dress at the premiere of *Four Weddings and a Funeral* in 1994. With her is star of the film Hugh Grant and Polygram Filmed Entertainment chief Michael Kuhn, while just chomping his way into the picture is Lord (Lew) Grade. Hugh is said to have received $100,000 for his starring role but this went up to £7 million by the time he filmed *Notting Hill* for the same company, with Julia Roberts

One of the great Hollywood stars and comedians, Phil Silvers happened to be in London filming *Carry on Follow That Camel*, when the invitation arrived to attend the James Bond premiere of *You Only Live Twice* in 1967

*The Greek Tycoon*. Anthony Quinn and his companion were in town for the launch of the film in 1967. Based on the story of billionaire shipping tycoon Onassis and Jacqueline Kennedy

Diana Dors was quite simply one of the most beautiful ladies I've ever photographed. She radiated warmth and affection towards everyone. At the time of this photo in the late 1950s she was one of Britain's biggest stars, and appeared in a string of top notch films including *A Kid for Two Farthings*, *The Weak and the Wicked* and *Yield to the Night*. She was also famously a Rank Charm School graduate and, like the other starlets, was often dispatched to towns and cities to open fetes, church halls, shopping centres and the like. A little later, having gained great success, she was invited to her home town of Swindon for a similar function. The local mayor was to introduce her to the masses. She had been born Diana Fluck, but understandably changed her name. Wanting to be careful on how he pronounced her former name, the mayor said: 'We have with us today a true star of our town. You may know her as Diana Dors, but we all knew her affectionately as Diana Clunt.' Diana dined out on that story for years. She died on 4 May 1984. Her only serious rivals from the glamour conscious 1950s had been dead for years – Marilyn Monroe in 1964 and Jayne Mansfield in 1967. Only Sophia Loren and Brigitte Bardot of the famous sex sirens have survived

© REX FEATURES

The hugely popular and talented Johnny Depp returns to London with the premiere of *Pirates of the Caribbean 2*. It went on to become one of the highest grossing films of 2006

Not one to be unescorted to a film premiere, Dudley Moore took along a cut-out of his wife, Suzy Kendall when she was unable to attend

© REX FEATURES

◀ OPPOSITE

This is one of my favourite pictures. It is of that great beauty Sophia Loren, taken back in 1957 when she attended the Royal Film Performance of *Les Girls*, in the presence of the Queen and Prince Philip. Sophia once famously said: 'I was so skinny I was given the nickname "Stechetto" – the stick. I was tall, thin and ugly – and dark like an Arab girl. I looked strange. All eyes. No flesh on my bones.' You certainly wouldn't recognise that description from my photo

On a lighter note, Sophia kindly agreed to pose with the Marx Brothers. I was asked to do this shot by director Michael Winner, who was supporting the boys in their revue at the Mayfair Theatre. Winner had put money into the show

© REX FEATURES

Anthony Perkins scared the wits out of me as Norman Bates in *Psycho* but in real life was an amiable and lively person as I have tried to show here

© REX FEATURES

They came … they saw … they conquered … the box-office tills across the world. Back in 1977, producer/director George Lucas took *Star Wars* from a blank page to Oscar-winning success, bringing together such talents as Harrison Ford, Dave Prowse, Peter Mayhew, Carrie Fisher, Mark Hamill and Kenny Baker in front of the camera

After years as a star of British and American films, it was *Star Wars* that made a fortune for Sir Alec Guinness. Producer George Lucas gave him 2.5 per cent of the net profits. Harrison Ford didn't do too badly out of the series, either. But I don't know about the little fellow, Kenny Baker

Growing into major stars. Tony Richardson with his daughters Joely and Natasha from his marriage to Vanessa Redgrave. They are pictured in 1974 at the *Dead Cert* film premiere

Five years on. Vanessa Redgrave is pictured at the premiere of *Agatha* with her daughter Joely Richardson and son Carlo Nero, from her association with Italian actor, Franco Nero

Before he found fame as 007, Timothy Dalton was an established actor and also consort of Vanessa Redgrave

© REX FEATURES

*Nightmare on Elm Street* brought Robert England to London to promote the film – complete with his exotic limb. That film was also to introduce Johnny Depp to the screen

© REX FEATURES

Three Hollywood greats came to London and I managed to capture them. Here are Charlton Heston, Clint Eastwood and Walter Matthau in relaxed mood at Brown's Hotel

BELOW
I'm with her. At the party following the Royal Film Performance of *The Three Musketeers*, zany Spike Milligan keeps Raquel Welch amused

© REX FEATURES

© REX FEATURES

ABOVE
George Clooney has built
himself a strong fan base in
the UK, spending a lot of
time meeting his fans. Here
he is seen signing autographs
at the premiere of *A Perfect
Storm*

Pierce Brosnan was to
become one of the most
popular James Bonds. Celine
Balitran is sandwiched
between him and another
great star, George Clooney

© REX FEATURES

© REX FEATURES

© REX FEATURES

© REX FEATURES

*Battlefield Earth* brought John Travolta to London. Earlier in his career he had studied dance under Fred Kelly, Gene's brother, and he went on to star in *Saturday Night Fever* and *Grease*

With hindsight, she might have squeezed a bit harder! Sadie Frost and her former husband, Jude Law

*Any Given Sunday* saw that great Hollywood actor Al Pacino visit London on a promotional tour for the film

© REX FEATURES

Peter Ustinov, later to be knighted, and Maggie Smith, later to become a dame, were just two of the stars to turn out for the star-studded *Evil Under the Sun*

OPPOSITE ▶

Flashback to the early days when the stars actually got dressed up for public appearances, Euan Lloyd, a film publicist who went on to become a successful producer, is pictured with Gregory Peck and his wife, Veronique, at the premiere of *The Sea Wolves*

© REX FEATURES

Jackie Chan backing Britain. Well-known martial arts expert, Jackie Chan was keen to pose in front of the Union Jack, on one of his visits to London

© REX FEATURES

**LEFT**
He went on to become one of the British cinema's biggest hell-raisers, but here is Oliver Reed during the early part of his career in 1960 at the premiere of the Hammer horror film, *Two Faces of Dr Jekyll*

**OPPOSITE ▶**
The sex kitten herself, Brigitte Bardot, was present at the Royal Film Performance in 1956 of *Battle of the River Plate*, attended by the Queen and Princess Margaret. Brigitte was in London, filming *Doctor at Sea* with Dirk Bogarde at Pinewood Studios

© REX FEATURES

Heart to Heart. Well-known television husband and wife team, Stephanie Powers and Robert Wagner, with his daughter Katie by Natalie Wood, enjoy an outing to a film premiere in London

© REX FEATURES

*Proof of Life*, Russell Crowe pictured at the Royal premiere of the film. Taylor Hackford, Helen Mirren's husband, directed

© REX FEATURES

I photographed Eddie Murphy, one of Hollywood's enduring stars, at one of his early successes, the premiere of *Beverly Hills Cop*

© REX FEATURES

Hammer horror veteran Vincent Price, is pictured with Veronica Carlsson

© REX FEATURES

**ABOVE**
Mrs Brad Pitt, otherwise known as Angelina Jolie, so loved working at Pinewood Studios on *Tomb Raider* that she bought a home nearby

**ABOVE RIGHT**
I wish I had captured Michelle Pfeiffer on my camera, but credit must go to my son, Scott, who has taken my place on the red carpet at London film premieres, now that I have retired

ABOVE

Nigel Havers and Ben Cross, pictured with their wives, at the royal premiere of *Chariots of Fire*, which preceded success at the Oscars. In his autobiography published last year, Nigel revealed that when *Chariots of Fire* was chosen as the Royal Film Performance he stood in line to be presented to the Queen Mother. 'Do you have double glazing?' she asked, leaving him lost for words

RIGHT

So nice to see you again. John Hurt receives a warm embrace from prankster Mel Brooks at a screening of *The Elephant Man*. Mel Brooks's wife, Anne Bancroft, starred in the film with Hurt, Anthony Hopkins and John Gielgud. I had to laugh once when I read that Mel Brooks, always the great comedian, said: 'We were so poor, my mother couldn't afford to have me. The lady next door gave birth to me.'

◄ OPPOSITE

Columbia film executives, Leo Jaffe, *left*, and Marion Jordan, *right*, mingle with stars Lesley Caron and Warren Beatty at the Royal Film Performance of *Born Free*. The Queen and HRH the Duchess of Kent attended the premiere at the Odeon Leicester Square in March 1966

© REX FEATURES

Maurice Chevalier, a great French entertainer, was still making films into his seventies. Here he joins assembled guests at the Royal Film Performance of *The Horse's Mouth* in 1959

This photograph of Sarah Miles was taken at a press reception for a film she was in, *Lady Caroline Lamb*, and she decided to give all of the assembled photographers and journalists in the Oliver Messel suite at the Dorchester a cabaret show. She was really off her rocker that day!

© REX FEATURES

© REX FEATURES

I was asked to join Henry Mancini at his scoring session for *Breakfast at Tiffany's* in London. I like this photo. It was taken without flash, hence it being a little less sharp than my usual photos

◀ OPPOSITE
Mohammed Ali and his daughter Jamilla arrive at Heathrow airport in London for the 1977 premiere of *The Greatest*. Columbia asked I meet them at the airport to get some photos for their publicity department, and later asked I attend the press reception at the Café Royal where Columbia's publicity director, Donald Murray, was sitting on the top table holding the baby. It was his job to look after Jamilla!

Vera Ellen and Joan Crawford at the royal premiere of *Battle of the River Plate*. They were chatting and I was keen to take a picture of them both, and asked if they might move a little closer to one another. Vera Ellen asked if I'd like them 'cheek to cheek'. I said, 'yes please'

© REX FEATURES

© REX FEATURES

Charles and Oona Chaplin,
in town making *Limelight*,
attended the royal premiere
of *Because You're Mine* in 1952

◄ OPPOSITE
At the premiere of *Rob Roy*,
I captured the great Gary
Cooper chatting with Dirk
Bogarde, Kenneth More and
Kay Kendall. He was one of
my childhood heroes. The
Queen had only recently
been crowned and Mr
Cooper was so nervous
about meeting her

This is a very interesting photograph, at the post-premiere party of *Battle of Britain* in 1969. I dubbed it 'The Best of Enemies'. It shows General Adolph Galland and Group Captain Douglas Bader sharing a joke. They were aces in opposing air forces during the war, and Galland was credited with 103 kills

© REX FEATURES

Jeremy Irons and Judi Dench join the irrepressible Sir Peter Ustinov for a chat at the premiere of *Evil Under the Sun* in 1982

◄ OPPOSITE
Three greats of the acting world, Albert Finney, Edward Fox and Tom Courtenay arrive at the Odeon in March 1984 for the premiere of *The Dresser*

The beautiful Gloria Swanson. Forever remembered
as Norma Desmond in *Sunset Boulevard*

# FIVE

# ROYALTY:
# A View from the Red Carpet

The first Royal Command Film Performance, in aid of the Cinematograph Trade Benevolent Fund, took place in November 1946.

Reflecting on the occasion, Harry Myers says: 'I was privileged to attend. I was just 18 years old and the film chosen was the wartime story, *A Matter of Life and Death* starring David Niven and Kim Hunter. Having cheated death, David Niven's character must argue with a celestial court to be allowed to carry on living.

'Hours before the arrival of the royal party, King George VI, Queen Elizabeth and the two young princesses, Elizabeth and Margaret, an unprecedented 50,000 fans jammed Leicester Square. The King was visibly shaken by this experience. The last 50 yards to the Empire Cinema took the royal party roughly 20 minutes. Film stars were marooned in the vast crowds. Women came limping into the foyer, shoeless, with their lovely evening dresses in tatters.'

Harry and his son Scott have photographed every Royal Film Performance in its 60-year-old history. They have been present for such films as *Scott of the Antarctic*, *To Catch a Thief*, *Romeo and Juliet*, *Lord Jim*, *Born Free*, *Close Encounters of the Third Kind*, *Kramer vs Kramer*, *Chariots of Fire*, *Die Another Day*, *Titanic* and *Star Wars*. Over the years, the famous red carpet at the Royal Film Performance and at other premieres attended by royalty, has been trodden by more famous actors, actresses and film-makers who could trump MGM's boast that it once had more stars on its books than there were in heaven.

The Royal Film Performance has been the principal fundraising event of the Cinema and Television Benevolent Fund for over sixty years. During that time King George VI attended five times and HM Queen Elizabeth II, who succeeded her father as patron, has so far attended thirty-one performances, including three as a Princess before her ascent to throne. The late Princess Margaret, an avowed film fan, was present at twenty-five RFPs, from the very first in 1946 to *Madame Sousatzka* in 1989. The late Queen Elizabeth, the Queen Mother, attended twenty RFPs.

Originally it was known as The Royal Command Film Performance but in 1949, at the request of Buckingham Palace, the word Command was dropped because it suggested the King had chosen the film.

In 1952 Her Majesty Queen Elizabeth II became Patron of the Fund and when it was re-constituted twelve years later to include the fast emerging commercial television industry, Her Majesty graciously signified her pleasure in continuing as Patron of the Cinema & Television Benevolent Fund. Over eighty years on the CTBF now spends around £1.3 million a year 'Providing Care Behind the Cameras' to workers in the British film, cinema, commercial television, cable and satellite industries. Funds raised by RFPs for the CTBF are significant and have so far exceeded £5 million with the 2002 and 2005 premieres of *Die Another Day* and *The Chronicles of Narnia: The Lion The Witch and the Wardrobe* raising £1 million alone. The 2006 premiere of *Casino Royale*, held in three cinemas in Leicester Square, raised in excess of £300,000.

In giving the Loyal Address on stage at the Odeon Leicester Square, Lord Attenborough, CTBF vice patron, said, 'I remember very well 60 years ago when King George VI inaugurated this annual event in support of the CTBF. In the years between we have enlarged everything and tonight there will be an audience in Leicester Square of over 4,200 – that has to be some kind of record.'

The primary home of the RFP has always been the Odeon Leicester Square, the venue for forty-six Royal Film Performances to date. Across the square, the old Empire Theatre hosted seven RFPs, whilst the new Empire has hosted three. The only other venues to be used are the Odeon Marble Arch, which stood in once, and the Royal Albert Hall for two recent premieres.

The Loyal Address, where a dignitary welcomes the Royal Patron, the audience, and the cast and crew, has been delivered by Lord (Richard) Attenborough, on three occasions. Other stars – Sir John Mills, Sir Donald Sinden, Dame Wendy Hiller, Toby Stephens, Sir John Gielgud and Hayley Mills – have made single deliveries. In 1954, for the first time, the audience inside the auditorium could see (on a special screen) via closed-circuit television, the stars being presented to the Queen in the line-up, albeit mute. In 1957 sound was added, and commentaries for both the audience and for national television were included – much to the chagrin of Harry, who later had a constant battle with director and friend, Steve Minchin, and his television lighting. The lighting Harry needed to take decent photographs was quite different from what the TV cameras wanted!

Royal Performances also became famous for the parties that followed the film's opening. These became more and more extravagant over the years. In the early days stars partied at hotels such as the Dorchester, Claridges or Grosvenor House. Many were lavish beyond belief. For *Die Another Day*, a Bond marquee with diamonds and ice was erected for 2,000 guests in Kensington Gardens, whilst after *The Chronicles of Narnia*, a magical winter wonderland was constructed for guests in Hyde Park where Turkish Delight was served. The latest, *Casino Royale*, had a casino-themed giant marquee housed in Berkeley Square and featured casino tables, vodka martini cocktails and delicious food!

## THE ROYAL FILM PERFORMANCES

| | | |
|---|---|---|
| 1946 *A Matter of Life and Death* | 1969 *The Prime of Miss Jean Brodie* | 1990 *Always* |
| 1947 *The Bishop's Wife* | 1970 *Anne of the Thousand Days* | 1991 *Hot Shots!* |
| 1948 *Scott of the Antarctic* | 1971 *Love Story* | 1992 *Chaplin* |
| 1949 *The Forsyte Saga* | 1972 *Mary, Queen of Scots* | 1993 *The Man Without a Face* |
| 1950 *The Mudlark* | 1973 *Lost Horizon* | 1994 *Miracle on 34th Street* |
| 1951 *Where No Vultures Fly* | 1974 *The Three Musketeers (The* | 1995 *French Kiss* |
| 1952 *Because You're Mine* | *Queen's Diamonds)* | 1996 *True Blue* |
| 1953 *Rob Roy the Highland Rogue* | 1975 *Funny Lady* | 1997 *Titanic* |
| 1954 *Beau Brummell* | 1976 *The Slipper and the Rose* | 1998 *The Parent Trap* |
| 1955 *To Catch a Thief* | 1977 *Silver Streak* | 1999 *Star Wars Episode 1: The Phantom* |
| 1956 *The Battle of the River Plate* | 1978 *Close Encounters of the Third Kind* | *Menace* |
| 1957 *Les Girls* | 1979 *California Suite* | 2000 *The Grinch* |
| 1959 *The Horse's Mouth* | 1980 *Kramer vs. Kramer* | 2001 *Ali* |
| 1960 *The Last Angry Man* | 1981 *Chariots Of Fire* | 2002 *Die Another Day* |
| 1961 *The Facts Of Life* | 1982 *Evil Under the Sun* | 2003 *Master and Commander: The Far* |
| 1962 *West Side Story* | 1983 *Table for Five* | *Side of the World* |
| 1963 *Sammy Going South* | 1984 *The Dresser* | 2004 *Ladies in Lavender* |
| 1964 *Move Over, Darling* | 1985 *A Passage to India* | 2005 *The Chronicles of Narnia: The Lion,* |
| 1965 *Lord Jim* | 1986 *White Nights* | *the Witch and the Wardrobe* |
| 1966 *Born Free* | 1987 *84 Charing Cross Road* | 2006 *Casino Royale* |
| 1967 *The Taming of the Shrew* | 1988 *Empire of the Sun* | |
| 1968 *Romeo and Juliet* | 1989 *Madame Sousatzka* | |

© REX FEATURES

The King and Queen arrive at the cinema for the first Royal Command film performance, Michael Powell and Emeric Pressburger's *A Matter of Life and Death*. The film edged out *The Magic Bow*, the story of Paganini, for the honour. On the left of the picture is Margaret Lockwood with her 5-year-old daughter Toots (Julia), who presented the bouquet to Queen Elizabeth. An 8-year-old Vanessa Redgrave presented a bouquet to Princess Elizabeth and 5-year-old Juliet Mills gave one to Princess Margaret. Royal, gold-painted armchairs were installed at the Empire for the royal party

© REX FEATURES

**ABOVE**
Huge crowds descend on
Leicester Square

The Queen greets comedian
Will Hay, just one of the
impressive line-up of nearly
forty stars who attended.
Standing next to Will Hay is
a favourite royal comedian
Bud Flanagan, with a young
Mai Zetterling by his side

© REX FEATURES

The Queen talks to
American star Joan Bennett,
while the King receives a
curtsy from one of England's
most enduring female stars,
Margaret Lockwood

© REX FEATURES

The popular American tenor Mario Lanza was the star of *Because You're Mine* in 1952 but didn't attend the royal premiere in London because he was under suspension from his studio MGM. However the stars still came out to shine – sixty-eight British and American stars stood in line. Here Queen Elizabeth II attending her first Royal Film Performance following the death of the King, meets an old friend Douglas Fairbanks Jr. On the right is James Hayter. He and I had previously met at a Butlin's holiday camp in North Wales when we were judges of a beauty contest

The Duke of Edinburgh accompanied Queen Elizabeth II to the premiere of *Because You're Mine* at the Empire Leicester Square and is shown greeting English actress Veronica Hurst. In the background is the immensely popular Hollywood star, Rock Hudson, while another stalwart of the British cinema, Mervyn Johns, father of Glynis, is in the foreground

© REX FEATURES

Princess Margaret at the premiere of *Because You're Mine*. A great film fan, she graced the Royal Film Performance on no less than twenty-five occasions. Incidentally, whenever Margaret attended a premiere, one of her conditions was that we later supply her with a set of 8 x 6 photographs from the evening

This is one of my favourite pictures of the Queen, taken at the 1953 Royal Film Performance of *Rob Roy*. Her coronation had taken place earlier in the summer. It really shows off her beautiful dress. In the line-up on the left are James Robertson Justice and Kay Kendall

In the early days the selection of the Royal Film alternated between British and Hollywood films. In 1953, the British-made film *Rob Roy*, the shortest-running Royal Film at 81 minutes, was set before the Queen who is here meeting Bob Woolff, MD of RKO Pictures. On the right is J. Arthur Rank, later Lord Rank, a great believer in British films and talent, whose studios at Pinewood contributed many successful films over the years. He also owned Odeon cinemas and consequently hosted the royal party at many premieres. In the background are Prince Philip, the Duke of Edinburgh, and the Queen's sister, Princess Margaret

© REX FEATURES

© REX FEATURES

1956. *The Battle of the River Plate.* This shot of Marilyn Monroe being presented to the Queen is not only one of my favourite pictures but it has also been reproduced all over the world, probably more than any other picture I've taken. The Queen is wearing a black evening dress by Norman Hartnell. Marilyn was in London filming *The Prince and the Showgirl* with Laurence Olivier. She was accompanied by her husband, playwright Arthur Miller. Needless to say her presence created tremendous excitement, not least when she removed her wrap to reveal an extremely low-cut gown. Though she was at the height of her profession and fame, my one enduring memory was of how very, very nervous she was as she waited to be presented. With her in the picture are far left Bernard Lee, A. E. Matthews, Victor Mature and on the right is Anthony Quayle

© REX FEATURES

1954 saw one of the most controversial Royal Films, *Beau Brummell*, which dealt with the Queen's ancestor, King George III. It was a surprise choice as I learned that *Seven Brides for Seven Brothers*, one of the classical musicals, had been offered to the selection committee. It starred Stewart Granger as the dandy Prince Regent and Robert Morley as the mad King George. Prince Philip asked Granger if he thought the film was 'all right for Her Majesty?' A somewhat embarrassed Granger replied: 'If you could manage to distract her attention when Robert Morley appears, it might be better, sir.' When cabinet papers were revealed thirty years later, they showed that the Queen had summoned the Prime Minister, Sir Winston Churchill, to complain. The Queen is seen shaking hands with American actor, Brian Donlevy. Also in the picture is Valentina Cortesa, who sobbed when she was presented. The Queen asked if she was well. 'I'm too emotional for this kind of thing,' she said. Others shown are Peter Finch, Mona Freeman and Stewart Granger, who borrowed money from me for the taxi fare, and Jean Simmons

Following the controversial *Beau Brummell*, the selection committee chose the risqué *Les Girls* for 1957. The Queen was later to announce that she would not be available for a Royal Film Performance in 1958 nor every single year henceforth as she wanted to spread her patronage more widely. One actor who was pleased to be present at the event was Leslie Phillips. He recently wrote in his autobiography: 'It was a great moment when *Les Girls*, my first Hollywood film, was shown to HM the Queen and Prince Philip. As it turned out I was the only member of the cast able to make it so I had Her Majesty all to myself'

Jayne Mansfield's famous assets caught the eye of Her Majesty when she was presented at the premiere of *Les Girls*. 'You are so beautiful,' the buxom American star told the Queen

There was no Royal Film Performance in 1958 but the following year Queen Elizabeth, the Queen Mother, and Princess Margaret attended the screening of *The Horse's Mouth*. Simone Signoret shook hands with the Queen Mother. Terry Thomas is on the left and Lord Rank is also in the picture. This was the last RFP at the old and magnificent Empire in Leicester Square before it was reconstructed

© REX FEATURES

The Duke of Edinburgh, without the Queen, honoured *The Last Angry Man*, in 1960. To the left is major Hollywood star Kim Novak. On the right is Vivian Cox. In the early days, the Royal Film Performance was on a Monday, so that stars could rehearse their part in the stage show that preceded the film. One such show saw John Mills, Tyrone Power and Montgomery Clift perform Noel Coward's 'Three Juvenile Delinquents'. Often, however, these stage efforts proved embarrassing and in 1953 were dropped. They were later revived in a more modest form by producer Vivian Cox.

© REX FEATURES

© REX FEATURES

The Queen Mother, accompanied by Princess Margaret and Antony Armstrong Jones attended the Royal Film Performance of the Bob Hope-Lucille Ball comedy, *The Facts of Life* in 1961.

© REX FEATURES

In 1964, the Queen was about to give birth to Prince Edward and the Duke of Edinburgh saw *Move Over Darling* without her. One of Britain's most popular actresses, Margaret Rutherford, was presented that year. Also in the picture are Stanley Baker, Honor Blackman, Leslie Phillips and far right, complete with moustache, is Richard Attenborough

© REX FEATURES

American star George Peppard meets the Duke of Edinburgh. Also shown are Samantha Eggar, Cliff Richard, Britt Ekland and the much admired Jack Hawkins. Most of the distinguished actor's films after 1966 had to be dubbed as throat cancer took hold. HRH Princess Alexandra attended a special memorial service to him, which was attended by such luminaries as Princess Grace of Monaco, Ingrid Bergman and Ann Todd. Addressing the audience that night, John Mills said, 'Although he couldn't use his own voice on the screen, his character and presence were stronger than at any time in his career'

Sean Connery looks on as his then wife Diane Cilento curtsies to the Queen Mother. Next to Sean is *Carry On* star, Sid James

A rare glimpse of royal affection in public saw the Queen receive an air kiss on the cheek from the Duchess of Kent. This I snapped outside the Dominion Theatre when *Battle of Britain* had a royal premiere back in 1968

**ABOVE**

The Queen wore some of her most spectacular jewellery and the ribbon and badge of the Order of the Garter for the premiere of *Born Free* in 1964. She is seen here talking with the popular stars, Virginia McKenna and Bill Travers, who played game wardens, Joy and George Adamson, in Carl Foreman's world-wide success, the story of Elsa, the lioness, in Kenya. I once went to their beautiful home for a photographic session. I was pleased to note they had no lions!

*Born Free* attracted a host of international stars, many from the star-studded James Bond spoof, *Casino Royale*, which was filming at the time. Seen here are Ursula Andress, Woody Allen, Raquel Welsh, and James Fox

Princess Margaret, seen here with her husband Lord Snowdon, was a huge film fan. She attended the very first in 1946 to *Madame Sousatzka* in 1989. I had had a rather embarrassing moment with a young Princess Margaret, back in 1952 at the premiere of *Because You're Mine*. In my rush to get one more photograph of the Queen as she left the Empire Cinema, I ducked under a crash barrier. As I came up, Princess Margaret brushed past and I very nearly went up her skirt. She turned around and laughed. A lovely and much missed lady. Having met Lord Snowdon at a socialite event when he was Antony Armstrong-Jones and unknowingly given him a tip about what exposure to use in his camera, I subsequently met him on many occasions, when he accompanied Princess Margaret to royal premieres. He obviously remembered our first encounter, as when walking down the royal line-up he would always stop when he saw me and shake my hand

Her Majesty meets
Hollywood stars William
Holden and Sophia Loren.
Jack Hawkins is in the
background

BELOW
Princess Margaret chats with
Richard Burton and Elizabeth
Taylor at the 1968 premiere
of Franco Zefferelli's *Romeo
and Juliet*

Italian star Gina Lollobrigida shakes Princess Margaret's hand at the premiere of *Romeo and Juliet*. Also in the line-up are Christopher Plummer and Mia Farrow, former wife of Frank Sinatra and partner of Woody Allen

© REX FEATURES

ABOVE

This was taken in available light as the television cameras present did not like flash photography. Danny Kaye was in town to be presented at this royal film, Zefferelli's *Romeo and Juliet*. On his left are Susannah York and Peter Ustinov. The Duke of Edinburgh is seen chatting to Joan Collins

The Queen meets Hollywood stalwart Karl Malden

© REX FEATURES

Joan Collins is presented to the Queen. Also in the picture are musical star Tommy Steele and Richard Chamberlain

A young Prince Charles meets stars Olivia Hussey and Leonard Whiting at the 1968 premiere of *Romeo and Juliet*, his first Royal Film

© REX FEATURES

Prince Michael of Kent meets Ava Gardner. Alongside her is Peter Sellers

© REX FEATURES

© REX FEATURES

Samantha Perkins is probably in her mid-40s now but back in 1969 she presented a bouquet to Princess Alexandra at the premiere of *The Prime of Mrs Jean Brodie*. This was the first X-rated film to be presented to royalty and a ten-second sequence featuring schoolgirls sniggering over a rude joke next to a nude stature was deleted, by order of the selection committee, to spare the royal party embarrassment. It was re-instated for the general public the next day. However news leaked of the cut on the evening of the premiere, causing Prince Philip to ask, rather curtly, the director Ronald Neame, 'Do you think we're all children? Removing a scene in case we're offended is really very silly'

*Funny Girl* was not a Royal
Film Performance but it did
attract royalty back in 1969.
Comedian and film star Peter
Sellers was enamoured of
Princess Margaret and they
are seen here at the
premiere

© REX FEATURES

They never really made it
internationally on the big
screen, but top British
comedians, Eric Morecambe
and Ernie Wise, were
national institutions because
of their television shows
which attracted millions of
viewers, particularly their
Christmas specials. On the
right is Rachel Roberts

© REX FEATURES

Don't make me laugh!
I didn't hear the joke but
Spike Milligan has the Queen
Mother in fits of laughter –
and also Christopher Lee –
at the premiere of *The Three
Musketeers*

© REX FEATURES

Hollywood star Barbra Streisand, in a flowing cloak, upstaged the Queen back in 1975 at the premiere of *Funny Lady*, by ignoring protocol and speaking first when being presented to Her Majesty. Since her arrival in London she had repeatedly asked why women had to wear gloves and men didn't at the royal occasion. She asked the Queen. The flustered Queen had no answer. Also in the picture are co-star James Caan and James Stewart. Behind Barbra Streisand is Jon Peters, who had been her hairdresser but later became a top film producer

Prince Charles shares a joke with Julie Andrews at the premiere of one of the *Pink Panther* films, as Herbert Lom looks on

© REX FEATURES

The Duchess of Kent is escorted to a premiere by Lord Louis Mountbatten and receives a soldier's guard of honour. Euan Lloyd, the producer, dedicated his later action film *The Sea Wolves* to Lord Mountbatten, after he had been murdered in Northern Ireland

© REX FEATURES

Princess Anne is introduced to Olivia Newton John, one of the brightest stars to come out of Australia, who went on to star with John Travolta in *Grease*. With her is Sir John Mills

BELOW
Superman meets the Queen Mum. Christopher Reeve, who had only one minor screen role before he was picked to play the famous comic strip hero, in London. Unfortunately, he was to die in 2004 after being paralysed in a riding accident in 1995

© REX FEATURES

© REX FEATURES

*Star Wars: The Empire Strikes Back* received a royal premiere in 1980. Princess Margaret led the royal party and is seen here being introduced to Carrie Fisher. Also shown are Sir Alec Guiness and Harrison Ford

© REX FEATURES

BELOW
Maggie Smith, Alan Alda and Donald Sutherland are introduced to Princess Anne

© REX FEATURES

© REX FEATURES

*For Your Eyes Only*. Princess Margaret and the Princess of Wales at the royal premiere of the 007 flick. It was Diana's first royal premiere

© REX FEATURES

I also photographed the radiant Princess Diana and Princess Margaret in colour at the premiere of *For Your Eyes Only*

OPPOSITE ▶

In 1985 the screening of John Brabourne's *A Passage to India* inaugurated British Film Year, and as a fully British epic production from a celebrated director, David Lean, it was the perfect title to launch a national campaign that helped cinema-going recover after the attendance nadir of 1984. The programme, attended by the Queen Mother and the Prince and Princess of Wales, also featured a medley of four of the Queen Mother's favourite songs, including 'We'll Meet Again'

**ABOVE**
A royal trio. Film fans
Princess Anne and the
Princess of Wales are
captivated by the Queen
Mother at the 1985 Royal
Film Performance, where *A
Passage to India* was selected
after its earlier success
opening British Film Year.
The film was produced by
John Brabourne, husband to
Lord Louis Mountbatten's
daughter, Patricia

*Empire of the Sun* (1988) was the second Steven Spielberg picture to be selected for the RFP, and featured Christian Bale as the youngster stranded by the Japanese invasion of Shanghai during the Second World War. Here I captured Princess Diana talking with the film's producer Jeremy Thomas. He had just won the 'Best Picture' Oscar for *The Last Emperor*

Prince Charles and Princess Diana attended the royal premiere of *Steel Magnolias* in 1990. They are seen here with actress Sally Field, Olympia Dukakis, who won a Oscar for her performance, and Julia Roberts

© REX FEATURES

© REX FEATURES

Princess Diana chats to Barbra Streisand and Nick Nolte at the royal premiere of *Prince of Tides* in 1991

Princess Michael of Kent and Odeon cinema manager, Chris Hilton. In the background is Prince Michael

Up until 1959, the Empire, Leicester Square hosted many premieres before it was renovated and split into three screens. It had opened in 1896 and here Prince Charles and Lord Attenborough mark the 100th anniversary of the cinema in 1996

© REX FEATURES

BELOW
**The Duke and Duchess of York**

◄ OPPOSITE
Not the most spectacular of royal films in 1996, but the controversial rowing film, *True Blue*, saw the Queen in a most spectacular blue dress for the premiere. In fact *True Blue* shouldn't have been the royal selection that year but *Evita* was delayed at the last moment

© REX FEATURES

Prince Charles and his younger son, Prince Harry, meet the talking parrot at the premiere of stage musical *Dr. Dolittle*

The Duke and Duchess of York and their children, Beatrice and Eugenie

© REX FEATURES

ABOVE
The Queen greets Jim Carey and his then girlfriend Renee Zellweger at the premiere of *The Grinch* in 2000. Looking on are director Ron Howard and producer Brian Grazer

© REX FEATURES

Pierce Brosnan is presented to HM The Queen in 2002 at the premiere of *Die Another Day*, the most financially successful Royal Film Performance to date

*The Chronicles of Narnia* took the Royal Film Performance away from Leicester Square in 2005 and cinema equipment was installed at the Royal Albert Hall to host the event. Prince Charles and the Duchess of Cornwall were the guests of honour at this the 59th Royal Film Performance.